MAX CAPACITY TRAINING

D1057574

Max Capacity Training

How Unconventional Workouts Can Turn Minutes Into Muscles

Samy Peyret

Intelligent Laziness Books
San Francisco, 2011

The information and advice contained in this book are based upon the re-search and the personal experiences of the author. They are not intended as a substitute for consulting with a health care professional. The publisher and author are not responsible for any adverse effects or consequences resulting from the use of any of the suggestions, preparations, or procedures dis-cussed in this book.

Cover designer: Leigh Anne Ference-Kaemmer
Editor: Ann Harshbarger

Copyright © Samy Peyret, 2011

All rights reserved. No part of this publication may be reproduced, stored in a retrieval system, or transmitted by any means, electronic, mechanical, photocopying, recording, or otherwise, without the prior written permission of the copyright owner.

ISBN 0-615-43546-7

To my brother

Contents

Contents

Introduction

HE UNFOLDED THE PIECE OF PAPER and read the first question out loud. "Rick seems to have lost a lot of weight recently. Is his health okay?" I was attending the quarterly all hands meeting at my company. With recent news of Steve Jobs taking a medical leave of absence at Apple, some employees were concerned that our own CEO's rapid weight loss might be due to health problems. Rick smiled. "There is no need to be alarmed," he said "I just decided to get in shape." He continued: "People often ask me how I did it but they're always disappointed by the answer… diet and exercise." The whole company laughed.

I met up with some friends that same evening and told them the story. "What do you think he meant by diet and exercise?" I asked. "Salad and jogging," one answered. "Screw that, I'd rather watch C-SPAN and iron my socks," continued another. That's what diet and exercise mean to most people: unsatisfying food and boring mindless movements. The truth is that you don't need to eat bunny food and jog an hour per day to become fit. It's a huge waste of time and frankly, a waste of life.

This book will teach you how to become fit efficiently. As a result, your looks will follow naturally. You will learn how to maximize your utility of time, your utility of exercise and your utility of food to optimize your results. You will read about how a group of people doubled their endurance performance with just ten minutes of exercise per week. You will discover how athletes boosted their power output by 17% while cutting their workout time by 67%. You will find out how a Japanese ice skating team lost 9 times more body fat in 15 weeks than their peers did in 21. We will go over three highly efficient workout protocols and 48 bodyweight exercises you can use to maximize your training capacity. You will learn the five fundamental rules to nourish your body properly and how to create your own meal plan. Finally, you'll uncover a few good tools to help you work out, eat properly and stay motivated once and for all.

Max Capacity Training is a no-BS way of getting results. If you're willing to commit an hour per week to applying the concepts of this book, I guarantee you will see great improvements in both your fitness aptitude and your body self-image.

PART I
The Right Mindset

Always Picked Last

"He who rejects change is the architect of decay.
The only human institution which rejects progress is the cemetery."
- Harold Wilson

G ROWING UP, I WAS ALWAYS PICKED LAST IN PE CLASS. It was fair; I sucked at every sport I tried. When I was thirteen, my parents enrolled me in the athletics team. After a year of training I participated in a regional 1k race. I came in last... by far. A coach from another team had to bring me water before I could even cross the finish line. I was young and training four hours a week, but my performance remained pathetic. But time kept ticking and life kept happening. I went to college, graduated and got a job. My interests started to shift and I began to favor a game of poker over a game of soccer. After all, I was a better competitor with my body sat down on a chair. Inevitably, I became a little chubby. Not even a year after graduation, my girlfriend's grandma, who had only seen me once before, noticed I had gained weight just by seeing me in the background of a photo. Man, it was bad. My friends all gained a good amount of weight too, so I figured it was just a normal part of growing older. On Black Friday of the following year, I went shopping with a friend. After walking for a mere thirty minutes, my back started to hurt. On Christmas day, my cousin challenged me to a push-ups contest. One, two, three, four, fi-uhm-fi… I collapsed. Worst of all, my sexual performance had been getting worse and worse. On the first night of January, my girl-friend and I were celebrating the New Year in bed. But my stamina was piss poor. "Oh, uhm, that's alright…" she said as I rolled to my side. Ugh! I knew it too. I sucked at anything and everything that required a physical effort, including sex.

That was the day something snapped in my head. I had tried the *laissez faire* approach, but it obviously didn't work. I had to do something because things weren't going to change on their own. So, I went to the library and checked out a couple of books. They were alright, but their advice really wasn't applicable to people who live in the real world. Going to the gym for two hours a day, five days a week? Come on! Not all of us workout for a living. I gave the books back and instead I started talking with my nutritionist friend. She knew a lot about food, but not so much about training. She recommended I met with athletes, gymnasts and fighters; so I did. They talked to me about muscle hypertrophy and protein synthesis. I had no idea what they were talking about so I picked up some textbooks and read research papers to get to the meat of what matters. The more I learned, the clearer I was able to define my goals. I needed to design a plan that would be doable for a normal person like me and that would make me considerably stronger. I narrowed it to three criteria:

- Takes a short time
- Can be done anywhere
- No weights, no equipment

It took a few trials and errors, but eventually I got it. I optimized my utility of exercise so much that I only train for sixteen to twenty-five minutes a day, three days a week. That's just about one hour of workouts per week total.

Just weeks after starting my new routine, people started to notice I had gained speed and stamina. I used to be the first to take a break when we played soccer, but now I could outlast all of my friends. My confidence shot up, and my body started to transform. My gut was fading away, and my abs were starting to show. Two months later, I participated in a local 5k race and placed in the top 3%. I hadn't even jogged since high school, but I still outran hundreds of people who actually had trained for that race! Then I started to do things I couldn't do before. On a trip to London, I walked all over the city for twelve hours straight, and my back didn't hurt. That same Saturday, I challenged myself and performed one thousand push-ups in half a day. And best of all, I became a much stronger lover.

I credit all these positive changes to the training program laid out in this book. I'm sharing everything with you, and I hope you will make the best of it.

ℬ · ℭ

Clear Your Mind

"In the spider-web of facts, many a truth is strangled."
- Paul Eldridge

BEFORE YOU GO ANY FURTHER, I suggest you completely clear your mind from everything you know about eating and exercising. There is so much misinformation out there that the best way for you to reach your goal is to purge everything you know and apply only the fundamentals. Forget about all the celebrity diets, home remedies and magic pills. These are all distractions that will keep you from reaching your goals.

Don't dwell on the details. They might be right or they might be wrong, but all they do is distract you from the big picture. "Should I eat white shell eggs or brown shell eggs?" It doesn't matter.

Surely, success and failure are not random. Nobody's born with superhuman strength, yet some of us can run the Iron Man while others can't walk a mile without pausing halfway through. We've all learned to walk, run, jump, push and pull. Can we not learn to become stronger and faster as well? Most people choose to live a sedentary lifestyle and let their bodies go to waste. A few of us prefer to take what we were given and make it better. The fact that you just picked up this book tells me that you are one of the latter. So clear your mind, stick to the fundamentals and get ready to do some hard work.

ຽ · ଔ

The Approach

"Efficiency is intelligent laziness."
- David Dunham

THERE IS SOMETHING YOU NEED TO UNDERSTAND ABOUT ME. You see, I am a lazy person. This doesn't mean that I try to avoid work at all costs, but rather that I only do the bare minimum in order to achieve my goals. The Max Capacity Training Program (MCTP) laid out in this book reflects this "laziness". There are multiple ways to gain strength; we could swim for an hour a day, or we could do two hundred sit-ups every morning. Both of these methods will develop strength, but they are not efficient. We need to use methods that take less time and give more results. In the end, it all comes down to the concept of utility.

You Need to Maximize Utility

A few summers ago, a friend of mine was going to move to New Mexico to work on a project for a few months. He asked me to take care of his tomatoes while he was gone. He instructed me to "water them every day, but just a little bit. Water the tomatoes enough but not too much." The first few drops of water are essential to the tomatoes' survival. If I gave enough water for the soil to be nice and moist, the tomatoes would grow bigger and taste better. If I added some more, the tomatoes would still be big and tasty, but the extra water would be wasted. Finally, if I added too much water, the tomatoes would die. When he told me to water them "enough, but not too much", my friend really asked me to maximize the tomatoes' utility of water.

Tomatoes

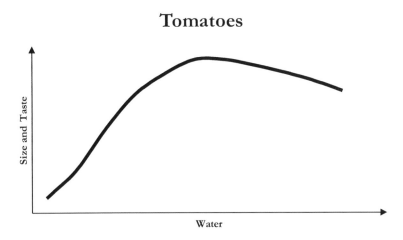

As we water the tomatoes, they become bigger and taste better. If we water them too much, they start to deteriorate.

Similarly, you need to feed your body a minimum of food to survive. Eat more, and it will grow stronger. Eat too much and it will grow weak again. The same is true for exercising. Exercise the right amount, and your body will grow strong. Exercise too much, and your results will be counterproductive.

Your Body

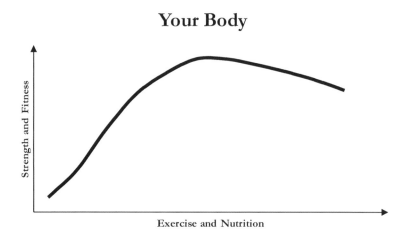

With the right amount of food and exercise, we can maximize our strength.

Our goal is to intake just enough of the right foods and to perform just enough of the right exercises to maximize our strength. Our time is valuable too, so for the sake of convenience, we want to keep our workouts short and effective.

Let's Keep It Convenient

We've all seen people go to their local gym, do one hour of weight lifting followed by another hour of cardio. You know what? I used to be one of those people. I would start by working out my arms with whatever dumbbells were available at the time. Then it was a game of cat and mouse to find a machine I wanted to use that wasn't already hogged up by somebody else. After an hour of that, I'd hop on a treadmill and jog an hour away like a soulless zombie. I did gain some strength and I did increase my endurance, but I hated it. I exercised for six hours a week, paid for a gym membership and spent twenty minutes in traffic each way just to work out. That was a reasonable way to gain strength, but it definitely wasn't convenient.

I think we can agree that unless you truly enjoy this kind of routine, it's clearly not the way to go. Instead, let's just do a quick workout, have fun with it and get back to our lives quickly.

First, we need to free ourselves from any specific location and equipment. This means no gym, no machines, and no free weights. I'm not saying that they're useless; they're just not right for our goals. How will we exercise then? Quite simply, we'll be using our own bodyweight. Every exercise in this book is bodyweight-only!

Oh, I can hear the "bodybuilders" grumble from here: "I'm never gonna gain strength with bodyweight exercises." Well, Mr. Bodybuilder, if you can perform ten consecutive one-handed handstand push-ups, you should be writing your cover letter to the Cirque du Soleil instead of reading this book. Bodyweight exercises are not only excellent for building explosive strength, but they are also very convenient. We can do them anywhere without any equipment.

Second, we need to free ourselves from time constraints. We can't spend two hours working out every day. Not only is the marginal utility of exercising for so long very low, it is also incredibly inconvenient. Instead, we will work at a VERY IN-TENSE rate for fifteen to thirty minutes every other day. That's about one hour per week. We just saved about ten hours' worth of our time. But make no mistake; our workouts will be extremely intense to make up for all that time we save.

Finally, we must eat convenient foods; foods that are quick to prepare and quick to eat. If you've looked at other popular exercise programs, you know that the people who designed them think you have no life. Cook a 4oz chicken breast at 10:00 am. Seriously?! Are you out of your mind, buddy? We've got other things to do at 10:00 am than cook ourselves some chicken. We need good foods we can eat on the go. We need nutritional guidelines we can commit to. This book provides just that.

ॐ · ॐ

Commit to the Max Capacity Training Program

"A man who wants to do something will find a way;
a man who doesn't will find an excuse."
- Stephen Dooley Jr.

JUST BEFORE TAKEOFF ON AN AIRPLANE FLIGHT, a flight attendant reminded boxing heavyweight champion of the world, Muhammad Ali, to fasten his seat belt. "Superman don't need no seat belt," taunted Ali. "Superman don't need no airplane, either!" replied the stewardess.

If you're going to do something for yourself, you might as well do it right. So, don't be a smartass and follow the rules. No excuses.

1. Work out on time, every time, at max capacity.

The MCTP's workouts can be done anywhere, at any time, without equipment and in about twenty minutes. What's that? You don't have twenty minutes to spare? Go to sleep twenty minutes later tonight. Done. Now you have enough time to exercise and you'll sleep better at night. You have absolutely no excuse to skip a workout… No, wait! You do have one excuse: injury. If you get injured, you should go see your doctor immediately. If you don't think it's worth seeing a doctor, then it's probably just all in your head. So unless you have a note from your doctor, you will work out. No free passes.

2. Follow the 5 principles of eating right.

I've seen it before: people start a strength-building program, keep all their focus on the exercises and completely dismiss nutrition. These people never achieve the results they set out for. Good nutrition is essential! The workouts described in this book will beat the crap out of your body. It's up to you to nourish it properly so it can recover in time for the next workout. You will need to follow a well-defined eating schedule and eat the right foods. Later in the book, you will find out exactly how to do that. You have to follow the guidelines if you want to see the results.

3. Log everything.

You are now embarking on a project, an experiment to transform your current body into a much stronger and leaner one. As with any experiment you will need to record your progress as it comes. You will record your weight, your body measurements, how many reps you did, how much water you drank, how many grams of protein you ate, etc… You will use this log to see how fast you've progressed in the past, tweak what you're doing in the present and forecast your results into the future. You will also use it to compete against yourself, to set yourself new goals or to adjust your workload. Throughout the book, I will introduce you to the tools you need to log your progress successfully.

℘ · ℨ

PART II
The Right Workouts

How to Build Muscles

"A jug fills drop by drop."
- Buddah

BUILDING MUSCLES IS SIMPLE, all you need to do is increase the amount of protein in your muscle fibers. Okay, so how can you do that? Your body is constantly destroying and creating muscle cells at roughly the same rate such that your muscles stay the same size. This is called homeostasis. The trick is to make your body build muscle cells faster than it destroys them. To do that you need two things: a way to toggle your body into creating a positive protein balance (that's what the lab rats call building muscle) and a way to nourish it enough amino acids to support the whole process[1]. The single most effective way to induce a positive protein balance is to exercise. But a workout without proper nutrition won't be enough to build muscles. You'll need a nice supply of amino acids in your blood to do that. You can think of your muscles as skyscrapers, exercise as construction workers and amino acids as building materials. If you want to build the Burj Dubai you're going to need plenty of workers and an abundance of materials. Having all the workers in the world without building supplies won't get anything done. Likewise, having a ton of materials with no workers isn't gonna help much. So to build muscles, you need to work out and eat proteins. Eating proteins is easy, but working out is a little ambiguous. Does it mean working up a sweat or exercising until you pass out? How much workout do we really need?

Back in 1994, Dr. Rooney et al. took 42 healthy people and assigned them to 2 groups. Both groups exercised with the same amount of weight, they both did the same number of repetitions and they all finished at the same time. The only difference is that one group plowed through the exercise without rest while the other group paused for 30 seconds in between reps. In other words, the no-rest group brought their muscles to fatigue while the other group didn't. After six weeks, Rooney found that, just by varying the rest time, the group that exercised to fatigue increased their dynamic strength by 33% more than their peers[2]! Lawton[3] and Tran[4] later confirmed these findings. So it's clear that, at the very least, we need to bringing our muscles to fatigue when we work out. But how far do we really need to go?

In the 70's, gym rats started to talk about exercising until muscular failure. Muscular failure is a fancy term that means working out until your muscles simply cannot pump out another rep. The idea is that if you reach muscular failure, then you've reached the ultimate state of fatigue, and that means bigger muscles. The concept is still around today and it's being parroted in every fitness forums and men's health magazines. Well, it turns out that bringing your muscles to failure just isn't necessary. Sorry, anonymous internet jock and fad-following magazine columnist, you're both wrong. Studies have found no significant difference between training to fatigue and training to failure[5].

Now we know that if we want to maximize our utility of exercise, we need to work out somewhere between fatigue and failure. The last hard reps are the ones that count.

Exercise

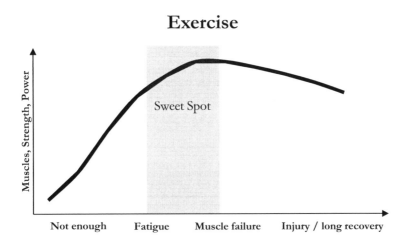

There are two ways to fatigue muscles: heavy weights or more volume in less time[6]. Since we're using bodyweight only, we'll induce muscle fatigue by doing more in less time: that means reducing rests. We call this workout density. We want a very high workout density.

Note that the exercises in this book are easy enough that you won't be building maximum potential muscles. So you won't look like a bodybuilder in the end, or as Clive James would say "a condom stuffed full of walnuts." However, you will develop useful strength and that will definitely show.

Push Harder for Faster Results

"And I always found that the harder I worked,
the better my luck was, because I was prepared for that.."
- Ed Bradley

IN 2007, DR. MARTIN GIBALA OF MCMASTER UNIVERSITY conducted a study on a group of healthy men and women. The group performed a total of 6 sessions of high intensity workouts for a total of 2.5 hours including recovery time. The workouts consisted of 30-second bursts of "all-out" sprint cycling against a strong resistance followed by up to 4 minutes of rest. Over two weeks, the candidates doubled their endurance when training at 80% aerobic activity, lasting 51 minutes as opposed to the initial 26. They also improved their racing performance by reducing the amount of time they needed to complete a 30km simulated cycle time trial by 10%[7].

A year later, Burgomaster conducted a similar study, this time comparing high intensity workouts to the more traditional, government recommended low intensity exercise. The experiment lasted 6 weeks. At the final test, the group that trained using the traditional low intensity method increased their peak power output by 7%. Not bad. Until you consider this: the group that exercised at high intensity increased their peak power output by 17%! That's more than double the increase of the low intensity group. Not only that, the high intensity group only committed 33% as much time to exercising as their peers, and most of it was just recovering.[8] If we only look at actual exercise time, the high intensity group worked for 10 minutes per week vs. 270 minutes for the low intensity group!

Similar studies have been conducted at other universities. In 1994, Dr. Tremblay of Laval University divided a pool of students into 2 groups. One group cycled for 30 to 45 minutes at a time, at low to medium intensity, 4 to 5 times a week for 21 weeks. The other group started with 30 minutes of medium intensity cycling and then switched to shorts bursts of high intensity exercise. They did that for 15 weeks. At the end of the experiment, the high intensity group lost 9 times as much fat in 15 weeks as the endurance group did in 21 weeks[9].

In 1996, Dr. Izumi Tabata had an endurance group exercise at 70% capacity for 5 days a week for 6 weeks. He also had another group, a high intensity group, train at max capacity for 8 rounds of 20 seconds work, 10 seconds rest. By the end of the 6 weeks, the endurance group increased their aerobic capacity by 10% and their anaerobic capacity stayed the same. The high intensity group increased their aerobic capacity by 14% and their anaerobic capacity by 28%. The high intensity group maximized their capacity and outdid their rivals by exercising for 40 minutes per week vs. 300 minutes for the endurance team.[10] We will pay homage to Dr. Tabata's experiment by adapting its protocol for our own needs later in this book.

Clearly, working at high intensity is more efficient than conventional training, and it maximizes the utility of both our strength and our time. For that reason, it is the perfect method to reach our goals.

Why does Intense Training Work so Well?

The International Sports Sciences Association, a certification agency for personal trainers, teaches two important rules they call the "Overcompensation Principle" and the "Overload Principle". The Overcompensation Principle simply explains that when you stress your body, it will respond by overcompensating. If you break a bone, your body will overcompensate and rebuild it stronger than before. Similarly, if you stress your muscles, your body will build them stronger so that they can support it in the future. The Overload Principle states that you must overload your body for it to adapt and improve. You must push yourself to do better if you want to progress; otherwise you'll just stay right where you are. Traditional aerobic exercises recommended by the government and the popular press do not follow either of these principles. Doing 45 minutes of elliptical at level 3 every day month after month does not overload your body and thus, your body doesn't need to overcompensate. On the other hand, training at high intensity is the exact opposite of conventional training; it forces you to overload your body, and your body then responds by getting stronger. Max Capacity Training takes full advantage of high intensity to build your body and to make you progress faster.

How to Workout at Max Capacity

Every day, at 8:30 am, I close the door to my apartment and walk a hundred feet to my car so that I can drive to work. On the rare days I'm not late, I see a young couple jogging and chatting as they pass me going the opposite direction. What these people are doing is not high intensity exercise. They are working at 50%-60% of their capacity. You, on the other hand, will be working at 90% to 100% capacity. You won't be able to discuss politics during your workouts... instead of talking, you will be panting like a dog. Your sweat will be dripping on the floor within the first five minutes. If it's not, you're not pushing yourself hard enough. By the end of your workout, your muscles will need so much oxygen that you will be light headed. If you're not, you are not pushing yourself hard enough. What does max capacity training mean? It means that you will exercise as hard and as fast as you possibly can, as if you were sprinting to win a race. You will need to keep pushing yourself hard as long as the timer is going or as long as you still have reps to perform. You will be performing at the maximum of your cardiovascular capacity. Just like the subjects of the McMaster experiment, you will give it all you've got.

₱ · ℛ

Before We Begin

"Success is neither magical nor mysterious. Success is the natural consequence of consistently applying the basic fundamentals."
- Jim Rohn

O N THE DAY I FIRST WENT SKYDIVING, the instructor sat me down and ran me through a small list of things I needed to know so that I would have a pleasurable experience and not die a terrible death. Today I'm doing the same with you. There are a few foundations you need to understand before you can start the MCTP. Don't worry, it won't take long.

Bodyweight Movements 101

You just rocked out to a Santana concert and you've decided that you want to learn how to play the guitar like a rock star. Carlos Santana has practiced playing the guitar for a long time before becoming the expert that he is today. Now, despite what your mommy told you, you're not special. If you expect to become an expert guitar player, you will need to practice. As a novice, your first step would be to learn the basics. How should I position my guitar? What is an E note and how do I play one? As you progress, you will learn to play chords, scales and finally, songs.

Your workout routine is no different. Since you are starting as a novice (see "Clear Your Mind"), you will need to learn and master the proper movements of the basic bodyweight exercises. How should I position my hands? My feet? What is the range of movement? Learning the basics will not only give you a good base to start with, it will also reduce the risk of injury when you move on to the more advanced workouts.

The basic bodyweight exercises include pushing (e.g. push-ups), squatting (e.g. squats), splitting (e.g. lunges), and core work (e.g. planks). Almost every other exercise found in here are variations of these four basics. You will find a description for each of them in Section IV. It is crucial that you become familiar with them before you start this program. So go on, skip ahead to Section IV and learn how to do the four basic moves. Try them out at your own pace and have someone verify your form. When you're done, flip back to this page.

Reduce the Risk of Injury

The Max Capacity Training Program is very intense, and if you don't do it right, you'll get hurt. The number 1 rule to reduce the risk of injury is FORM OVER SPEED. If your form is off, slow down or pause! You will always be better off going a little slower with good form than going fast with sloppy form. You will enjoy better results and stay injury free. Do the exercises as fast as possible with good form. The other way to make sure you stay injury free is to warm-up your muscles before you start each workout.

Warming Up, Stretching and Cooling Down

A full workout always starts with a warm-up. The goal is to raise your body temperature and increase your pulse to an aerobic level. When you warm-up your body, you're reducing muscle viscosity. This means that your muscles can contract and relax faster, and as a result, you're improving your power output and efficiency. Your blood vessels dilate, so you can give your muscles more of the oxygen they need to work. You're working up a sweat that's essential for cooling you down so that you don't overheat during the workout. Most importantly, by warming up, you're significantly reducing your chances of injury[11]. There's a handful of good warm-up exercises, but the most versatile one is the one you haven't done since high school: Jumping Jacks. This one will get your blood flowing quickly. Researchers also advise that you warm-up the specific muscles you'll be working that day. That's the reason why, if you go to a tennis match, you'll see the players exchange some balls for 10 minutes. They're not practicing; they know how to hit a ball. They're warming up the specific muscles they'll be using for the game. So the official Max Capacity Training warm-up consists of two stages: jumping jacks to raise your body temperature and the exercises of the day to warm-up your muscles. Take it slow, there's no need to push yourself at this stage yet.

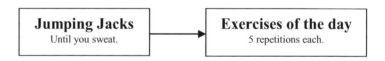

Fitness leaders all agree that a good warm-up is essential to a workout. Stretching, on the other hand is a lot more controversial. Some studies claim that stretching is beneficial, others conclude it doesn't do anything, and even some determine that stretching can cause more harm than good. Personally, I don't stretch and I'm doing just fine. I encourage you to do your own research about stretching and choose for yourself whether it's right for you. If you decide to stretch, always do it *after* your warm-up. Holding stretches before the muscles are warm is begging for injury[12,13]. Depending on your preference, you can plan your workout as one of the following:

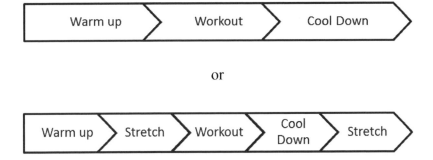

or

As you've noticed, your workout is always followed by a cool down period. The purpose of the cool down is to slowly decrease your pulse rate and lower your body temperature. It's essentially a reverse warm-up. All you need to do is keep moving. Don't seat your ass in the couch yet, walk around, take out the trash, do some chores. Cooling down will get rid of your muscle lactic acid faster than resting. In other words, it promotes faster recovery. Cooling down also prevents blood pooling so it reduces the risk of dizziness and reduces your chance to be sore for the next three days.

You're No Fish

Remember to breathe! If you don't, you'll pass out. Seriously. I've caught myself holding my breath in the final efforts of an exercise. It's dangerous. I've seen many others do it and you're probably no exception. You need to consciously check your breathing from time to time.

Just as importantly, you need to breathe properly. I only learned how to breathe when I was in my twenties. Nobody had ever taught me how. Breathing is simple on paper but it's tricky in practice. Here's how you do it:

1. Exhale as you're exerting force
2. Inhale as you're returning to your starting position.

Why don't you give it a try? Get on the floor and perform a push-up. Inhale as you lower your body to the ground. Exhale as you push yourself back up into a plank position. Repeat. If you're doing a squat, inhale as you lower your body into a sitting position and exhale as you push yourself back up.

Why should we breathe this way and not the other way around? Well, you want your muscles to have as much oxygen as possible to do their work. That's why you need to inhale before your muscles need the oxygen to push you up. If you start to inhale at the same time as your muscles start to work, they'll be at a deficit, and much of the oxygen will be wasted.

꽁 · ꝏ

Max Capacity Workouts

*"Scaling the mountain is what makes
the view from the top so exhilarating."*
- Dennis Waitley

THE WORKOUTS IN THIS BOOK ARE DESIGNED TO SCALE TO
anyone's fitness level. Whether you are an overweight
couch potato or an Olympian, the program adapts to your fitness level and will kick your ass regardless of who you are. It
doesn't discriminate.

How the Workout Plan is Setup

The goal of the workout plan is obviously to get you fit, but it's
also to keep you interested. For that reason, you will never do
the same routine twice. Sure, you'll still repeat your exercises,
because you need to get familiar with them, but you will perform them with a different goal every time. So, how do we do
that? It might sound complicated the first time you hear it, but
it's actually quite simple. Have a look at the table on the next
page.

Pool 1		Week 1 (Fifty-Ten)	Week 2 (Tabata)	Week 3 (T-Attack)
Day 1	Squats	33	...	... : ...
	Push Ups	12	...	
	Lunges	30	...	
	Plank Bridge	37	...	
REST 1 DAY				
Day 2	Elevated Push Ups	...	...	... : ...
	Bird Dog	...	...	
	Squat Pulses	...	...	
	Superman	...	...	
REST 1 DAY				
Day 3	Squat Touch Reach	...	...	... : ...
	Reverse Lunges	...	...	
	Drop Squats	...	...	
	Plank	...	...	

The MCTP is made up of 4 pools. This is Pool #1. All pools have the same structure: there are 3 weeks per pool, 1 protocol per week and 3 workout days per week. So you'll get 9 workouts per pool. Each workout consists of 4 exercises performed under that week's specific protocol.

On your first day, you will be doing the workout of Day 1 of Week 1: that's squats, push-ups, lunges and plank bridge according to the Fifty-Ten protocol. When you're done, log your score (we'll go over that in a bit) and take the next day off. The following day, work on Day 2 of Week 1 and so on. Once you've completed Week 3, you will start Week 4 in Pool #2. The first week of each pool introduces you to new exercises, but the protocols stay the same: Fifty-Ten, Tabata, and Time Attack.

1. Fifty-Ten Protocol.

How it works: There are 4 rounds. For each round, perform the maximum numbers of repetitions of each exercise in 50 seconds before going to the next. Go at your own pace, but be consistent. There are 10 seconds of rest between exercises. The total workout time is 16 minutes.

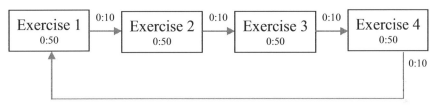

REPEAT 3 MORE TIMES

Example: On Week 1, Day 1, go for your maximum number of squats. Do as many as you possibly can in 50 seconds. You can pause if you need to, but the clock keeps ticking. When the 50 seconds are up, take a 10-second rest, then drop to the floor and start doing push-ups. When the 50 seconds are up, take another 10-second rest, then do as many lunges as your muscles will allow you. Finish your 50 seconds, take your next 10-seconds rest, then put yourself into a plank position. Hold your plank with good form until you no longer can. Rest for a final 10 seconds., then do it all over again for 3 more rounds.

Tip: You'll most likely be pretty tired by the end of the first round already, but it's important that you keep pushing! That's how you'll get results. If you need a break, take it, then go right back into it. You won't be able to do all these exercises without pause for 16 minutes. Not the first time you do them anyway. It's normal to take breaks, but try to keep them to a minimum.

Logging your performance: Record only the number of reps you were able to complete for each exercise on your first round (round 1).

Logging Example: On Week 1, Day 1, Round 1, my roommate performed 33 squats, 22 push-ups, 36 lunges and held his plank for a total of 37 seconds. He wrote his numbers down in the workout log sheet. He will reference them on Week 3.

Tools: If you're working from home or with your mobile phone, you can use the free Fifty-Ten Timer at *www.MaxCapacityTraining.com/fifty-ten.html*. You can also buy an interval timer enabled watch or a standalone timer. A popular one right now is the Gym Boss.

2. Tabata Protocol.

How it works: This protocol is based on the famous study by Dr. Tabata. For each exercise, work for 20 seconds and rest for 10 seconds. Repeat 8 times for a total of 4 minutes per exercise. After the 8th rest, move on to the next exercise. Total workout time is 16 minutes.

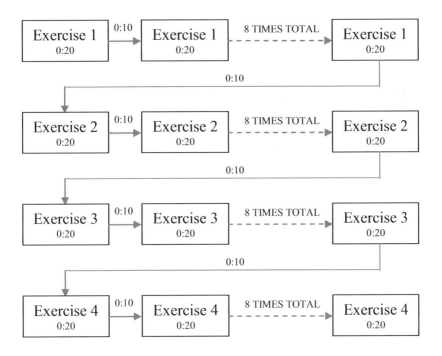

Example: On Week 2, Day 1, start by doing your 20 seconds of squats. Pause for 10 seconds. Repeat seven more times. At your eighth pause, get ready for some push-ups. When the ten second rest is up, get to work. Push-ups for 20 seconds, rest for 10 seconds. Repeat for another 3 minutes and 30 seconds. Lunges for 20 seconds, rest for 10 seconds. Repeat again. Make sure to keep the intensity high during your whole workout. Finally, after you eighth round of lunges, get ready to plank. Plank on for 8 rounds of 20 seconds and rest for 10 seconds.

Tip: Keep the intensity high, but pace yourself enough to be able to finish the exercise. If you can perform 20 push-ups in the first round, but can't do any in the sixth round, try limiting yourself to 15 push-ups instead, that way you will be able to finish all 8 rounds.

Logging your performance: Record only the lowest number of reps you were able to complete for each exercise.

Logging Example: On Week 2, Day 1, my roommate performed 12 push-ups, followed by 11, 10, 10, 8, 7, 6, 8. The lowest number of push-ups was 6 so he wrote 6 on his MCTP workout log sheet. His lowest number of squats, lunges and planking were 12, 15 and 10 seconds, respectively. Note that he only wrote down his lowest score, not his last.

Tools: You can use your own interval timer capable watch or you can visit *www.MaxCapacityTraining.com/tabata.html* from your computer or smart phone.

3. Time Attack Protocol.

How it works: For this workout, instead of performing the maximum numbers of reps in a specific time, you're going to do a specific number of reps in *minimum* time. For each exercise, add your score from Week 1 with your score from Week 2 and multiply the result by 3. That's your reps goal for the day. You can do your exercises in any order, jump from one to the other at any time and take rests whenever you want. Your mission is to complete all your exercises as fast as possible. Kudos if you can make it in less than 16 minutes.

$$\left(\begin{array}{c} \text{Week 1} \\ \text{Score} \end{array} + \begin{array}{c} \text{Week 2} \\ \text{Score} \end{array} \right) \text{X } 3 = \boxed{\begin{array}{c} \text{Week 3} \\ \text{Goal} \end{array}}$$

Example: On Week 1, Day 1 my roommate's scores were 33, 22, 36 and 37 for squats, push-ups, lunges and planking, respectively. On Week 2, his scores were 12, 6, 15 and 10. So on Week 3, Day 1, my roommate performed (33 + 12) x 3 = 135 squats, (22 + 6) x 3 = 84 push-ups, (36 + 15) x 3 = 153 lunges and (37 + 10) x 3 = 141 seconds of plank bridge. Then he did it again for one more round. He took rests only when he needed them, both during and in between exercises.

Tip: Don't go too fast. Instead, try to save time by pausing less. Don't count reps with bad form. If you're having trouble, gather yourself for a few seconds and try again.

Logging your performance: Record the total time it took for you to finish your workout, pauses included.

Logging Example: On Week 3, Day 1, my roommate completed the circuit in 16 minutes and 59 seconds. This is the number he wrote on his log sheet.

Tools: Any watch will work for this exercise. You can also visit *www.MaxCapacityTraining.com/time-attack.html* from your computer or smart phone.

Scheduling Your Workouts

The easiest way to stick to your workouts is to schedule them at a time that works for you. Remember to keep at least one day of rest between workouts.

My good friend works out on Monday, Wednesday and Friday mornings. He rests on Tuesday, Thursday, Saturday and Sunday. I prefer to do my exercises on Sunday morning, Tuesday evening and Thursday evening after work. I rest on Monday, Wednesday, Friday and Saturday. So go ahead and choose something that works for you. Choose a schedule that you can stick to. Worse comes to worst, you can always switch up your schedule, as long as you put in three days of workouts per week.

When I first started, I used a free service from a website called *RememberTheMilk.com* to remind me that I had to work out. Every Sunday, at 9:50 am, Remember The Milk sends me a text message on my cell phone: "Workout in 10 minutes". I also get the same message at 6:20 pm for my 6:30 pm workouts on Tuesday and Thursday. If you already have you own scheduling system, be it Outlook or anything else, make sure to add in your workout sessions! If you don't have one, you can sign up for a free account at *www.RememberTheMilk.com*. Make it a habit because habits are hard to break.

Pushing Harder (Optional)

Here's a quick way to push harder during your workout. The Fifty-Ten and Tabata protocols give you 10 seconds of rest time between sets. To push harder, instead of resting for those 10 seconds, hold your position.

Standard: 50 seconds of squats, rest for 10 seconds, 50 seconds of push-ups, rest for 10 seconds…

Harder: 50 seconds of squats, hold the squat for 10 seconds, 50 seconds of push-ups, hold it down for 10 seconds…

ട്ര · ൽ

PART III
The Right Nutrition

My Fat Friend

"If only it were as easy to banish hunger
by rubbing the belly as it is to masturbate."
- Diogenes the Cynic

M Y FRIEND IS FAT. He's a mid-twenties guy of average height who weighs over 210lbs. So one evening, I handed him a sheet of paper and asked him to write down what he ate and drank that day. This is what he gave back to me:

Time	Food	Calories
8:00 am	Nutri-Grain Strawberry flavored cereal bar.	140
12:30 pm	Chicken Lean Pocket and Weight Loss Shake	480
4:00 pm	Pop Corn and Diet Coke.	130
7:00 pm	Beef Portobello Lean Cuisine.	210
7:30 pm	Skinny Cow Low Fat Fudge Bar.	100

Two things jump out right away. First, he ate just over 1,000 calories, clearly not enough for a man of his size. He deprived his body of the food it needs and was victim of the fat gain associated with very low calorie diets (VLCD)[14]. The second thing that stands out from this list is that all the foods he ate were labeled as "diet friendly" low fat, low sugar healthy choices. The reality is that these foods are all processed crap. They have almost no nutritional value, and they're loaded with chemicals neither of us even knew existed.

The next day I went to his brother, a thirty-six year old man of average height with a six pack of abs that would make Calvin Klein models jealous. I handed him a sheet of paper and asked him to write down what he ate and drank that day.

Time	Food	Calories
8:00 am	Oatmeal, whole milk, banana. Mushroom omelet. Coffee.	600
10:30 am	Greek yogurt and strawberries. Hot tea.	200
1:00 pm	Steak burrito. Grapes. Water.	630
7:30 pm	Chicken breast, 3 tomatoes, black beans, rice, apple, peach. Water.	700

See the difference? The guy with the six pack of abs ate roughly 2,100 calories, twice as much as the fat guy. He gave enough food to his body. And not only was his diet well balanced, it was exclusively whole foods. No processed junk. There are a few other important differences between the two diets. My fat friend only hydrated his body twice in the whole day with a can of Diet Coke and a "weight loss" shake. His well-toned brother on the other hand regularly drank tea and water with every meal. My fat friend ate half of his daily calories at noon, but his brother spread out his caloric intake throughout the day.

These brothers have very different bodies for a reason, and something tells me it's not genetics. One is eating properly and the other isn't. So let's eat like the guy with the nice abs and avoid eating like my fat friend.

℘ · ℚ

The 5 Principles
of Eating Right

"We are living in a world today where lemonade is made from artificial flavors and furniture polish is made from real lemons."
- Alfred E. Newman

W E CAN EASILY BREAK DOWN THE STRONG BROTHER'S DIET into five fundamental rules. Write these down on a piece of paper that fits in your wallet. Every time you're about to put food in your mouth, pull out your little note and make sure that it passes the five fundamental principles of eating right. Here they are:

1. Drink a lot of water
2. Don't drink calories
3. Eat balanced meals
4. Eat the right amount
5. Eat natural, unprocessed foods

These rules are simple and easy to understand. If you follow some of them, you might see improvements. If you follow all of them, you *will* see improvements, whether you want to lose weight, gain weight or don't care either way.

Rule #1: Drink a Lot of Water

In 329 BC, Alexander the Great led his army across the Bactrian desert. 75 kilometers away from any water source, his soldiers were dying of thirst. A Macedonian scout approached the emperor, kneeled down and offered him a helmet-full of water. "Is there enough for 10,000 men?" asked the king. The scout shook his head. Alexander took the helmet with one hand and, with a stern look, poured every last drop in the sand.

Fortunately, you're not a desert crossing emperor leading a thirsty army, so you get to drink as much water as you want. In fact, while you're doing Max Capacity Training, you *need* to drink about 0.8 fluid ounces of water per pound of bodyweight.

An easy way to calculate how much water you should drink is to take your bodyweight in pounds and divide it by 10. That's the number of glasses of water you should drink in a day.

$$\frac{Bodyweight\ (Lbs)}{10} = Cups\ of\ Water$$

For example, I weight 170lbs, so I need to drink 170 / 10 = 17 glasses of water per day.

Don't drink all your water in one swoop. Not only is it ineffective, it's also dangerous! So spread it out. Sip on water throughout the day. Here's a good trick I learned from a professional fighter. Tomorrow morning, bring a 1 gallon jug of water to work and set it on your desk. Use it to fill and refill your cup throughout the day. Every time you finish your cup, fill it up again, even if you're not going to drink it right away. Your challenge is to finish the jug before you get in your car to go home.

Rule #2: Don't Drink Calories

If you want to lose fat, liquid calories are the second worst thing you can ingest, after poison. Let me show you what I mean. Remember my fat friend? Here's what his Weight Loss Shake is made of:

Nutrition Facts

Serving Size Custom Food 325g (325 g)

Amount Per Serving

Calories 230   Calories from Fat 20

% Daily Value*

Total Fat 2g	3%
Saturated Fat 1g	3%
Trans Fat	
Cholesterol 0mg	0%
Sodium 360mg	15%
Total Carbohydrate 44g	15%
Dietary Fiber 4g	16%
Sugars 38g	
Protein 10g	

Vitamin A	35% •	Vitamin C	100%
Calcium	40% •	Iron	15%

*Percent Daily Values are based on a 2,000 calorie diet. Your daily values may be higher or lower depending on your calorie needs:

		Calories	2,000	2,500
Total Fat	Less than		65g	80g
Sat Fat	Less than		20g	25g
Cholesterol	Less than		300mg	300mg
Sodium	Less than		2,400mg	2,400mg
Total Carbohydrate			300g	375g
Fiber			25g	30g

Calories per gram:
Fat 9   •   Carbohydrate 4   •   Protein 4

When he looks at the label, he sees "230 calories" so he figures that this is a healthy low-calorie meal replacement. What he doesn't see is this: "Sugars 38g". These numbers don't mean much by themselves, so let me put them in terms of real food. My fat friend's "weight loss" shake has about the same nutritional value as three bites of canned tuna and ten sugar cubes! Does that sound healthy? Seriously! Would you have that for lunch? The worst part is that he already knows this stuff doesn't work. He's been drinking it for years now, and he's been gaining weight the whole time. Stay away from weight loss drinks; they're rubbish!

You already know you shouldn't drink soda and beer, so let's not waste time talking about these. What you might not know is that every other alcohol is just as bad. When my friend decided he would get in shape, he started replacing beer with straight vodka, thinking it was the healthier choice. Less calories, perhaps? But then he saw this:

1 bottle of beer:	130-150 calories
1 shot of vodka:	100 calories
1 shot of tequila:	100 calories
1 glass of Coke:	94 calories

He quickly realized that on Thursday night happy hours, he'd been drinking the equivalent of 8 to 10 glasses of Coke in a span of a few hours. In comparison, nutritionists recommend that you drink 0 glasses of Coke… ever.

Alcohol is nothing more than fermented or distilled sugar. When you drink it, your body metabolizes it almost instantly into fat. So unless you're going to hibernate for the next few months, it's not helpful to your cause.

Now, there are other liquid calories that sound healthy but that you should stay away from. Orange juice, or any other fruit juice. It's delicious and full of vitamins, it comes from a fruit, so what's wrong with it? The reality is that when the factory processes the oranges, all the vitamins get stripped away and they then have to add them back. Also all the fiber from the fruit is lost. And finally, it's liquid calories. So skip the fruit juice and eat the real thing instead. If you're just dying for fruit juice, make it yourself but drink it with moderation. Of course, every rule has an exception. While almost every calorific drink will give you counterproductive results, milk can help you stay on track. Milk contains two of the highest quality proteins you can get: casein and whey. In a 12 week study, researchers compared the effects of drinking milk or a sports drink on building muscles and fat loss. One group was given 2 cups of skim milk immediately post workouts and another serving 1 hour after. The other group was given the same number of calories with a Gatorade equivalent. Both groups followed the same resistance training program. At the end of the 12 weeks, the sports drink group gained 5.3lbs of muscle and lost 1lb of fat. By contrast, the milk drinking group gained 8.8lbs of muscles and lost 2 lbs of fat! The milk drinkers gained 60% more muscle and lost twice as much fat[15]. All this to say "don't drink liquid calories," but milk is cool.

Rule #3: Eat Balanced Meals

My colleague walked into my cube one morning. He leaned against my desk and said "Samy, I'm gonna eat nothing but Edamame for lunch for the next 30 days." I laughed in his face. If you don't know, Edamame is a soy bean you can find in most Sushi restaurants. I'm not sure what he was trying to get out of this, but it certainly didn't seem well thought out. "I'll bet you $20 you can't do it," I challenged. "Okay, I'll do it just to show you!" he answered as he walked back to his cube... He gave up on day 3. I'm sharing this with you because his Edamame challenge is a lot like those grapefruit-and-an-egg diets. They're just plain stupid. They're also un-sustainable. Even when money's at stake, these things just don't work. We naturally need to eat balanced meals.

Every day, we eat three types of macronutrients: proteins, fats, and carbohydrates. These are the nutrients that provide us with the energy we need to live. All three are digested in the intestine, where they are broken down into their basic units: proteins into amino acids, fats into fatty acids and carbohydrates into sugars. Your body uses these basic units to build the substances it needs for growth, maintenance and activity.

Eat Your Proteins

Protein is especially important for you because you are engaged in an intense physical training program. You need enough protein to grow and maintain your muscles and connective tissues. You'll find most of your proteins in meats, poultry, fish, eggs and milk. Sure, you can also find proteins in beans, nuts and grains but they're incomplete by themselves. They lack some of the amino acids your body needs and that means that you need to combine them to get complete proteins. Anyway, it's complicated and I'm way too lazy to look into it. So if you're a vegetarian or *gasp* a vegan, I suggest you pick up a book on vegetarian bodybuilding, I'm sure they explain all that stuff in there. As far as this book is concerned, though, protein comes from animals.

It's easy to choose your protein; you only need to lookout for two things:

1. Watch out for mercury
2. Watch out for saturated fats

Mercury is a poison. It's both natural and man-made. It falls with rain, goes in rivers and seawaters, small fish eat it, big fish eat smaller fish and we eat the fish. Bigger fish contain more mercury than smaller fish because they've been around longer and eat more of it. Mercury won't hurt you in small quantities but can make you sick if you eat too much of it. The FDA recommends that you stay away from high mercury fish such as shark, swordfish, albacore tuna, king mackerel and tilefish. However, feel free to eat low mercury seafood such as chunk light tuna, shrimp, salmon, pollock, tilapia and catfish.

Saturated fats are the other enemy. They're the ones that will increase your cholesterol, risk of heart disease and stroke. I'll show you how to identify them in a bit. You'll find saturated fats in fatty red meats, poultry skin and pork. It's important that you choose wisely and go for the lean cuts and trim all the visible fat out.

I use the list below every time I go grocery shopping to help me find some healthy proteins for my next meals. Most of the ingredients in this list will give you 20g to 35g of protein and under 2g of saturated fat per 100g serving. Don't try to figure out which one's the leanest and meanest, just go for whatever you're in the mood for:

GOOD SOURCES OF PROTEIN

Mammals:

Bison Ribeye Lean
Bison Top Round
Bison Shoulder Clod
Elk Round
Elk Tenderloin
Beef, Eye of Round
Beef, Top Round
Beef, Tip Round
Beef, Tri-tip
Beef, Flank
Beef, Brisket
Beef, Bottom Round Roast
Beef, Ground 96/4
Beef, London Broil
Beef, Top Sirloin
Game meat, Moose
Goat meat
Veal, Leg
Veal, Shoulder arm
Veal, Shank
Veal, Sirloin
Rabbit
Deer, Top Round
Deer, Tenderloin
Lamb, Leg
Pork, Cured Ham
Pork, Leg Sirloin

Pork, Tenderloin
Pork, Shoulder
Pork, Top loin

Seafood:

Salmon
Tuna, chunk light
Cod
Red Snapper
Carp
Mahi Mahi
Crab
Herring
Monkfish
Perch
Skate
Anchovies
Butterfish
Calamari
Pollock
Haddock
Catfish
Whitefish
Scallops
Herring
Rock Lobster
Sole

Shrimp
Clams
Tilapia
Oysters
Sardines
Trout
Eel

Dairy & eggs:

Eggs
Egg whites
Milk, Whole
Milk, 2%
Cottage Cheese
Greek Yogurt

Poultry:

Turkey Breast, skinless
Chicken Breast, skinless
Emu, top loin
Ostrich, Tip trimmed
Ostrich, Top loin

BAD SOURCES OF PROTEIN		
Mammals:	**Seafood:**	**Dairy & Eggs:**
Sausages	Albacore tuna	Cheeses
Bacon	Swordfish	Egg yolk
Hot Dogs	Shark	Non-fat dairy
SPAM	Other high mercury fish	
Bologna		**Poultry:**
Beef jerky (high sodium)		Chicken thighs
80/20 ground beef		Poultry skin
Other processed deli		Duck
meats		

If you're wondering about a food that you can't find in this list, make sure you look it up on *http://nutritiondata.self.com*. This website has a ton of useful information about any ingredient you can think of.

Eat Your Fats

This one's easy to remember. You can eat 3 types of fats: trans fats, saturated fats and unsaturated fats.

Trans fats are essentially hydrogenated vegetable oils. They're great for food manufacturers because they make their food last longer and they can be heated repeatedly (think French fries at the local fast food joint). However, trans fats are bad for you. They have absolutely no positive effect on your body. They increase your bad cholesterol and clog your arteries. You'll find trans fats in fast foods and packaged foods. Sometimes you'll see a box of crackers that claims "0g trans fat". What that really means is "this product contains less than 0.5g of trans fat per serving, but it does have trans fats." Even half a gram is too much. Long story short: stay away from trans fats.

Saturated fats are kind of a mixed bunch. They increase both good and bad cholesterol. They're easy to identify because they're solid at room temperature (like butter, the fat around a pork chop or the marble in a fatty cut of beef). You will inevitably eat some saturated fat throughout your day; *just try to keep it as low as possible.* Trimming the fat off your meat and passing on the chicken skin will go a long way.

Unsaturated fats are the good stuff. Not only are they good for your blood pressure and cholesterol level, they also help speed up your muscle recovery. You'll find unsaturated fats mainly in plant products. *Try to restrict almost all your fat intake to unsaturated fats.*

GOOD SOURCES OF FATS (UNSATURATED)

Nuts:	Seeds:	Other:
Macadamias	Sesame seeds	Peanuts
Hazelnuts	Sunflower seeds	Peanut butter
Pecans		Almond butter
Almonds	**Oils:**	Olives
Cashew	Flaxseed oil (uncooked)	Avocado
Brazilnuts	Olive oil	Salmon
Pistachio	Canola oil	Sardine
Pine nuts	Soybean oil	Trout
Walnuts	Sesame oil	
Chestnuts	Sunflower oil	

NOT SO GOOD SOURCES OF FATS (SATURATED)

Lard	Cream	Animal fat
Butter	Cheese	Chicken skin
Mayonnaise	Ice cream	

BAD SOURCES OF FATS (TRANS)

Fast foods	Fried foods	Shortening
Packaged foods	Margarine	

Eat Your Carbs

Carbohydrates are fuel for your body. They give you the energy you need to move around and do well on your Max Capacity workouts. On a chemical level, we can divide carbohydrates into two groups, simple carbs and complex carbs, depending on how many carbon atoms they're made of. The popular view used to be that complex carbs are healthier than simple carbs because they get digested slower in our bodies, and thus they provide us with a steadier stream of energy throughout the day. Turns out that this isn't entirely true, so in 1981 Dr. David Jenkins introduced the concept of the glycemic index (GI)[16]. The glycemic index ranks foods based on how fast they are digested in the body. The slower the digestion rate, the lower the number, the faster the digestion rate, the higher the number. The recommendation, originally for diabetes patients, was to eat only low GI foods. Some fad diets, like the South Beach diet, popularized the concept for weight loss. However, research tells us that following a low glycemic index diet doesn't help with weight loss at all. In fact, after having reviewed nine studies, the American Dietetic Association strongly recommends against a low glycemic index diet for weight loss "since it has not been shown to be effective in these areas."[17] In 1997, Dr. Willett of Harvard expanded the concept of the glycemic index and introduced the glycemic load (GL). Now I'm not going to go into details on how the GL works, but suffice it to say that it won't help you any more than the GI if you're hoping to lose weight[18].

What's my point? Often times you'll come across a dietary concept that seems sound on paper but that fails to deliver results once it's tested in the real world. So, don't waste your time wishing that all those fancy schmancy acronyms will turn you into a super model. What really counts when choosing your carbs is the amount that you ingest. You'll learn exactly how much carbs you should eat per day in the next chapter.

For now, you just need to understand that some foods contain a lot more carbs than others. We'll call this carb density, and you can use it to your advantage when planning for your meals. If you find that you're naturally eating too much carbs, replace some of your high carb density foods with low carb density foods. On the other hand, if you're eating too little carbs, add some carb-dense foods to your diet for an easy way to reach your carbohydrate goals. For example, here are eight different ways to get 50g of carbs:

50g of Carbohydrates
1 Starbucks brownie
1 cup of white rice
1½ cups of kidney beans
2 apples
2 cups of Corn Flakes
25 tomatoes
2.5 lbs of sauerkraut
3 lbs of spinach

Generally, baked sweets like cookies and cakes are more carb-dense than grains such as rice, pasta and bread. Grains, in turn, are more carb-dense than legumes such as beans, which themselves are denser than fruits. Fruits, finally, contain more carbs than vegetables. So if you're eating too much carbs, try to eat more fruits and veggies. Conversely, if you're not reaching your calorific goals, eat more grains and legumes.

CARBOHYDRATES

Grains:
Amaranth
Barley
Bread, white
Bread, whole wheat
Breakfast cereal
Buckwheat
Bulgur
Couscous
Flaxseed
Millet
Muesli
Pasta, White
Pasta, Whole wheat
Oatmeal
Pita bread
Pop Corn
Quinoa
Rice, brown
Rice, white
Rice, wild
Rye
Spelt
Tortillas
Wheat
Wild rice

Legumes:
Black beans
Black-eyed peas
Chickpeas
Kidney beans
Lentils
Lima beans
Navy beans
Pinto beans
Split peas
White beans

Fruits:
Apples
Apricots
Avocados
Bananas
Blackberries
Blueberries
Cherries
Coconuts
Dates
Figs
Grapefruit
Grapes
Guavas
Kiwis
Lemons
Limes
Lychees
Mangoes
Melons
Nectarines
Oranges
Papaya
Peaches
Pears
Pineapple
Plums
Prunes
Raspberries
Strawberries
Tangerines
Tomatoes
Watermelon

Vegetables:
Acorn squash
Artichokes
Arugula
Asparagus

Beets
Bok choy
Broccoli
Brussels sprouts
Butternut squash
Cabbage
Carrots
Cauliflower
Celery
Collard greens
Corn
Cucumbers
Eggplant
Fennel
Green beans
Green peas
Hubbard squash
Kale
Lettuce
Mesclun
Mushrooms
Mustard greens
Okra
Onions
Parsnips
Peppers, green, red or yellow
Potatoes
Pumpkin
Radishes
Spinach
Sprouts
Sweet potatoes
Tomatoes
Turnips
Watercress
Yams
Zucchini

Rule #4: Eat the Right Amount

When I was researching proper nutrition I read all kinds of rec-ommendations. "Eat small meals five to six times a day.", "Eat only low glycemic load foods.", "Eat a bag of pork rinds once a day to get good proteins." I heard these claims everywhere: from popular programs, to fitness magazines, to blogs and even from gym rats. Naturally, I looked into it; but once I under-stood the science behind those claims, I realized it was all bull-shit. Whether you eat six times a day or three times a day doesn't change anything[19]. Eating low glycemic load foods over high glycemic load foods won't make you thinner or stronger[20]. The proteins in pork rinds are incomplete and use-less to our bodies. So I say go ahead and eat whenever you want. Don't worry about the glycemic load and eat pork rinds only if you want to. What really matters is that you *eat enough, but not too much.*

How Many Calories Should You Ingest?

The rule of thumb is to eat for your target bodyweight. Don't worry about your current bodyweight. If you want to weigh 160lbs, eat like a person who weights 160lbs. If you want to weight 220lbs, eat like a person who weights 220lbs. Makes sense, doesn't it?

How much should you eat then? To find out, simply multi-ply your target bodyweight by 12. So if you want to weight 180lbs, you would eat 180 x 12 = 2160 calories. This is the standard guideline for people performing the MCTP. Of course, everybody's a little different, but this is a great com-mon baseline. Because you'll be logging your body measure-ments, you'll be able to adjust your calorific intake once you're deeper into the program. Until then, 12 is the number to re-member.

Breaking Down Your Calories

Now that you know how much you should eat as a whole, you need to figure out how much of each food group you should eat. Here's a quick way to find out.

Proteins: *Eat your target bodyweight in grams.* If your target bodyweight is 180lbs, eat 180g of protein. 1g of protein contains 4 calories, so multiply your number by 4 to find out how many calories that makes. That's 180 x 4 = 720 calories from protein.

Fats: *Eat one third your target bodyweight in grams.* For a target bodyweight of 180lbs, eat 180 / 3 = 60g of mostly unsaturated fat. 1g of fat contains 9 calories, so multiply your number by 9 to find out how many calories that makes. That's 60 x 9 = 540 calories from fat.

Carbohydrates: *Eat your target bodyweight times 1.25 in grams.* E.g. For 180lbs bodyweight, eat 180 x 1.25 = 225g of carbs. 1g of carbs contains 4 calories, so multiply your number by 4 to find out how many calories that makes. That's 225 x 4 = 900 calories from carbs.

Checking the math, 720 calories of protein + 540 calories of fat + 900 calories of carbs = 2160 calories. We calculated 2160 calories earlier with the rule of thumb. Perfect. Calorie wise, this gives us a ratio of roughly 33% proteins, 25% fats and 42% carbohydrates. Now, remember that these are just guidelines. They're handy because they're easily calculated, but you don't have to be spot on every time. Give yourself a buffer of ±50 calories for each food group.

If you work out or play a sport in addition to following the MCTP, for every two hours of weekly training, add one time your target bodyweight to your total daily caloric intake. So, if you follow the MCTP and play ice hockey two hours per week, you would add two times your bodyweight to your daily caloric intake. For a target weight of 180lbs and 2 hours of ice hockey per week, your daily caloric intake would be 180 x (12 + 1) = 2340 calories.

Making It Easy

Let's face it, looking at nutritional labels and counting calories is a pain in the ass. It takes time and there's too much room for error. Thankfully, there are some nice tools out there that can do that for us, and they're free too. My favorite one is LiveStrong.com's Daily Plate from the Lance Armstrong Foundation. *LiveStrong.com* is a website that allows you to plan and log what you eat. The beauty of it is that it already knows the nutritional content of every food you can buy, so you don't have to look at the labels anymore.

Type in your food in the search box, say 'oatmeal', and LiveStrong will give you a list of popular oatmeal brands. Simply select the one you bought and add it to your log. Repeat for everything you plan on eating that day. Once you're done, the website will display a pie chart that breaks down your calories by protein, fats and carbs.

Daily Nutrition Breakdown

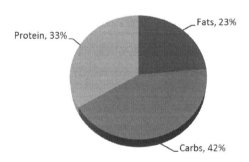

Fats, 23%

Protein, 33%

Carbs, 42%

Unfortunately, LiveStrong's legal team has been taking its sweet time to give me the rights to publish a screenshot of their website, so I just went ahead and made a mock-up of the pie chart they offer on their website. It is a very handy tool you can use to quickly see where you stand and adjust your meals if necessary. LiveStrong.com has apps for popular smart phones, so you can log your food while you're on the go. A bunch of other websites do the exact same thing, so find one you like and stick with it.

Rule #5: Eat Natural, Unprocessed Foods

The final rule of eating right is to eat natural foods. It sounds very inconvenient, but it's not that bad at all. Today, almost every food we buy is processed. Think about what you ate for breakfast this morning. Cereals? Maybe toast, a waffle, or some pancakes? Or even worse, maybe you didn't even have a breakfast this morning. What about lunch? Did you eat at a deli or a fast food joint? Did you have white rice or pasta? These are all unnatural foods. We invented all of these things; our bodies were never designed to eat them.

In the early 1900s, a controversial doctor named Weston Price studied the diets and the overall health of many different cultures all around the world. After two decades of research, he concluded that many of the diseases of modern countries (headaches, muscle fatigue, cavities, heart disease, tuberculosis, cancer, etc...) were not present in cultures that had diets based on natural foods[21]. Why? Because when a food is processed, it loses some of the essential nutrients that we need.

Though you don't have to buy organic ingredients, you should stay away from processed foods. So how do you know what's natural and what's processed? What you should buy and what you shouldn't? Two tips:

Shop in the side aisles.	If it comes in a box, it's processed.
In your grocery store, that's where you'll find all the fresh fruits, vegetables, fish, meat, eggs and milk.	Think frozen dinners, mac n cheese, hot pockets, instant ramen, cookies, etc...

For some of my friends, switching to natural foods was a breeze, but others had a hard time. For the scope of this book, your challenge is to eat just one non-processed meal per day. Whatever you want it to be, whenever you want it to be. All you need to do is eat one natural meal per day.

For the sake of convenience, you'll still be eating processed foods. When that's the case, make sure all the ingredients are natural. You'll be surprised at the differences you can find between products that otherwise look very similar. Let's have a look at the ingredients in store bought apple sauce:

Mott's Harvest Apple Cause: Apples, Water, Calcium Lactate, Calcium Gluconate, Ascorbic Acid (Vitamin C)
Santa Cruz Organic Apple Sauce: Apples.

Pretty big difference, huh? Now check out peanut butter:

JIF Reduced Fat Peanut Butter: Peanuts, Corn Syrup Solids, Soy Protein, Sugar, contains 2% or Less of: Salt, Molasses, Fully Hydrogenated Vegetable Oils, Rapeseed, Cottonseed and Soybean)Magnesium Oxide, Ferric Phosphate, Zinc Oxide, Niacinamide, Copper Sulfate, Pyridoxine Hydrochloride, Folic Acid.
President's Choice Peanut Butter: Peanuts.

So whenever you buy processed foods, make sure to have a look at the ingredients before you hand over your dollars.

Should I Take Supplements?

Max Capacity Training is very demanding on your body and you might find it difficult to reach the dietary goals we just talked about. So you could be considering nutritional supplements to give your body the energy it needs. This is a controversial issue amongst most fitness experts; some love them, some hate them. In the end, the choice is yours, and it's your decision to make. Here's my take on the issue.

Your goal is to stick as much as possible to the 5 principles of eating right. Try as hard as you can to reach your carb, protein and fat goals by eating only natural foods. If you can't make one of your goals, then you should start looking into supplements. Supplements offer no added advantage to your body, they're just here for your convenience.

My guess is that you'll face difficulty reaching your protein goal. Carbs and fats shouldn't be a problem. If you can't eat all your proteins by sticking to real foods, then you should seriously look into supplements such as protein bars, whey protein or soy protein. Unfortunately, these supplements are processed foods, so they're not the best but they're still better than nothing. *Only take supplements if you can't reach your calorific goals from natural foods.*

By the way, protein bars and protein powders are the only supplements I would eat or drink. Creatine, Nitric Oxide, Myostatin and all that other stuff pros take is useless until you can follow the 5 rules of eating right consistently. And my bet is that once you start following the 5 rules, you won't want to ingest any of that stuff anyway. The same goes for fat loss pills, which are pure crap. They only make your heart race to increase your metabolism. Stay away from this shit! I'm getting a little carried away here... As I said before, this is a personal choice; you need to decide for yourself.

℘ · ℭ

PART IV
Get Motivated

Conquer the Yoyo Effect

"Energy and persistence conquer all things."
- Benjamin Franklin

I GOT A TRAFFIC TICKET THIS PAST FEBRUARY. I was on my way home from a road trip when an officer clocked me above the speed limit, pulled me over and handed me a yellow slip. I calmed down instantly. I set the cruise control for the remaining two hundred miles and drove very carefully, constantly checking my rear view mirror. The following day, I made sure I never went above the speed limit. I counted at stop signs: one Mississippi, two Mississippi, three Mississippi. I even used my turn signal ten seconds before I changed lanes. This went on for a while, but soon enough I started to slack off again. Today I got another traffic ticket. Speeding. We're in the first week of June, it's not even been 4 months! After the officer handed me the yellow slip, do you know what I did? I set the cruise control. One Mississippi, two Mississippi,...

This is the Yoyo effect. One day, you get a wake-up call: you've been doing something wrong and it's time to correct it. So, you correct it. That lasts for a little while, but one time you kind of mess up. And before you know it, you're doing everything wrong again. It takes another wake-up call to set you straight. But you're going to fail again...

Everybody experiences the Yoyo effect. For me, it's speeding. For some people, it's flossing their teeth. For others, it's smoking cigarettes. In this book, of course, I'm talking about the Yoyo effects associated with nutrition and exercise. If you want to beat the Yoyo effect, you need to stay motivated all the way through and stick with all the elements of the MCTP. If you stick with it long enough, it'll become a habit and you'll be doing everything right without even trying. That's how you'll get the results you want. So, try to stay strong during the whole program and don't slack off. The program is fun, quick, and it's diversified enough that you'll be able to push through it both physically and mentally. The first step you should take to protect yourself from the Yoyo effect is to get rid of the obstacles that are in your way.

Get Rid of Obstacles

"One half of knowing what you want
is knowing what you must give up before you get it."
- Sidney Howard

IT WAS SUNDAY AND NOTHING INTERESTING WAS GOING ON that weekend. That's the day my other roommate (that's right, I have three roommates. Jealous?) decided he was going to get in shape once and for all. He took a trash bag, dragged it along the floor to the fridge and started filling it up with all the garbage that he used to think was food. Pizzas, French fries, Coke cans, beer, chicken nuggets, hot dogs, ice cream, ranch dressing... He threw all of it in the bag. He even threw some of my stuff out, that bastard. Then he went to the pantry and did the same thing. Nutella, potato chips, corn chips, popcorn, cookies, crackers, candy, pancake mix... He was not going to eat any of this stuff anymore, so there was no point in keeping it. He threw it all away. He also bagged some of the canned foods and gave them away to a local charity.

If you are serious about getting fit, get rid of all the temptations you have laying around. That stuff does not nourish your body, and it's in the way of your goals. So, throw all the junk away; you aren't going to eat it anyway.

℘ · ℛ

It's a Virtuous Cycle

"Affirmation without discipline is the beginning of delusion."
- Jim Rohn

I'VE READ A FEW BESTSELLERS that claim that if you stand in front of a mirror every morning and repeat an affirmation nine times, then inevitably it will come true. "I will take my body to its absolute best." The more you do it, the easier it will come. They call this the daily affirmation technique. Personally, I don't know what the hell those people are talking about. I only stand in front of a mirror to make sure I don't cut myself shaving. Something tells me that looking at your own reflection and talking to yourself isn't going to grow your muscles all that much. So, in good conscience, I can't recommend that you practice daily affirmation. Instead, let me give you a concrete case of "The more you do it, the easier it will come." The more you work out and nourish your body, the bigger your muscles grow. I think we can all agree here. The bigger your muscles grow, the higher your metabolic rate increases, the more fat you burn, the less dead weight you have to move around and the easier it is to work out. In other words, it just keeps getting easier as you go.

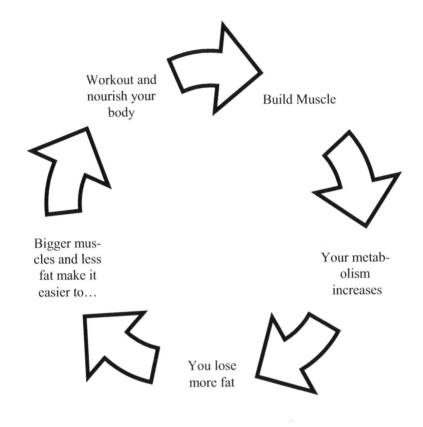

Workout and nourish your body

Build Muscle

Bigger muscles and less fat make it easier to…

Your metabolism increases

You lose more fat

So if one day you're really not in the mood to follow the plan, just remember that the longer you stick to it, the easier it becomes.

℘ · ℭ

Remind Yourself That You Sit On Your Ass All Day Long

"If it weren't for the fact that the TV set and the refrigerator are so far apart, some of us wouldn't get any exercise at all."
- Joey Adams

IF YOU'RE A 9 TO 5 PERSON LIKE ME, you spend 8 hours a day sitting at your desk. When it's time to go home, you sit behind the wheel of your car and drive for half an hour. Then you open the front door, drop off your bag and go sit on the toilet for a little while[i]. When you're done with that you turn on the TV, flip open your laptop and sit on the couch for another two to four hours. Finally, when the night is over, you move around for a little bit and go lay down in bed.

You spend less than 10% of your day being active, and when I say "active" I'm being generous. So the next time you don't feel like working out, remind yourself of how much time you've spent sitting that day and compare that with the 20 minutes of workout you're trying to avoid. You know, you're not going to get fit sitting down.

℘ · ℘

---

[i] My editor noted "This is a little gross, and I think unnecessary." I thought her comment was funny so I kept it in the final version. That'll show her!

Do It with a Friend

"It is better to be in chains with friends,
than to be in a garden with strangers."
- Persian Proverb

WHETHER YOU WORK OUT ALONE OR WITH A FRIEND won't change a thing about your progress, but it will make a world of difference vis-à-vis your motivation. I always invite my friends to train with me and in return, they invite me back. It's not just a workout anymore; it's a regular social event. Some of us are in better shape than others and vice-versa, but we all go at our own pace, we push ourselves as far as we can go and we help each other. We don't turn it into a competition; we make it into a team effort. Nobody finishes first. If one of us is lagging, the others will join back in and we'll all complete the workout together. We laugh, we grunt, we sweat, and in the end, we're happier than when we started. So find a friend or two, motivate them, lend them this book and get to work!

80 · CB

Turn Up the Tunes

"If music be the food of love, play on."
- Duke Orsino

MY FRIENDS AND I USED TO EXERCISE IN SILENCE because we didn't have a speaker system. One hot summer day, we were pushing through the second half of a Fifty-Ten workout and, man, it was hard. The heat was beating us down and we were on the verge of giving up. My upstairs neighbor, who's normally an obnoxious prick, saw us in our pain and shouted "Hey, let me help you guys out!" He ran up the stairs and disappeared. We could hear him through the ceiling as he was fumbling around in his apartment. During the 10 second pause, my friend looked at me as if to ask "What on earth is your neighbor doing?" Then, at the exact moment we started our third round of burpees, we heard a loud noise coming from above. "Stomp, stomp, clap. Stomp, stomp, clap." My neighbor was blasting Queen's "We Will Rock You" at maximum volume. Bad ass! We all looked at each other and smiled. This one song gave us a huge boost in motivation, and we doubled our efforts for the rest of the session. That afternoon, we went to Fry's and bought ourselves a set of speakers. To this day, we play music every time we work out. It makes training feel a lot more like a party than an actual workout. Try it, and see if it works for you.

You might have heard that music can boost exercise performance, but that's only a half truth. In a 2006 study, Dr. Yamashita found that individuals who exercise at a low intensity while listening to music had a lower rating of perceived exertion when compared to their friends who exercised without music. However, that observation didn't hold true for those in the group that trained at a higher intensity (60% VO$_2$max)[22]. So, that's not gonna work for us. On the other hand, researchers agree that music can be very motivational when exercising. They conducted a bunch of experiments to find out which type of music and tempo works best, but these were all in vain. If you're going to listen to music, choose music that you like[23]. If you like dance music, don't put on Metallica or Snoop Dogg. Play whatever you want. My favorite website to listen to workout music is _www.GrooveShark.com_. It's free and they have everything you can imagine. If you have a computer with you when you work out, make sure to check it out.

Measure Your Progress

"Don't pay any attention to what they write about you.
Just measure it in inches"
- Andy Warhol

THE THREE RULES OF THE MCTP are to work out at max capacity, follow the 5 principles of eating right and to log everything. Measuring your progress is a part of logging everything. You're already recording how many reps you perform and how long it takes you to perform them. Now you need to record information about your body. Seeing progress is a great motivator. Below is a table of the criteria you should jot down.

Measurement	Unit
Resting heart rate	Beats Per Minute (bpm)
Weight	Pounds (lbs)
Waist	Inches (in)
Chest	Inches (in)
Bicep	Inches (in)
Buttocks	Inches (in)
Thighs	Inches (in)

To avoid statistical noise, you should only record the above information once every 3 weeks, the first day of each new pool of workouts. Any more than that is overkill. Make sure you are consistent in your measuring.

Sometimes you'll find that you didn't make any progress. When you find yourself in this situation, ask yourself why that is. Did you skip workouts? Did you push yourself hard enough? Did you use good form? Did you drink your gallon of water a day? Did you eat too much? Not enough? Keeping a good log helps you catch your failures earlier rather than later. The sooner you unmask your problems, the sooner you can correct them.

ℰ · ℛ

PART V
The Workout Plan

Pool 1 – Schedule & Exercises

Here are the exercises you will be performing for the first three weeks. Write down your initial body measurements and log your results on this page as you complete the exercises.

Pool 1		Week 1 (Fifty-Ten)	Week 2 (Tabata)	Week 3 (T-Attack)
Day 1	Squats	…	…	… : …
	Push Ups	…	…	
	Lunges	…	…	
	Plank Bridge	…	…	
	REST 1 DAY			
Day 2	Elevated Push Ups	…	…	… : …
	Bird Dog	…	…	
	Squat Pulses	…	…	
	Superman	…	…	
	REST 1 DAY			
Day 3	Squat Touch Reach	…	…	… : …
	Reverse Lunges	…	…	
	Drop Squats	…	…	
	Plank	…	…	

Body Measurements					
Resting heart rate	…	Chest	…	Buttocks	…
Weight	…	Left bicep	…	Left thigh	…
Waist	…	Right bicep	…	Right thigh	…

Day 1: Squats

Position your feet just a little over shoulder-width apart with your arms relaxed at your sides. While keeping your torso up, lower your body until your thighs are parallel with the ground. At the same time, bring both your hands up in front of your torso. Keep your back straight the whole time. Come back up to your starting position to complete the move. Inhale on your way down, exhale when you push yourself back up. Add a score of 1 every time you cycle from the starting position to the ending position and back to the starting position. If you perform 10 squats, write 10 on your log sheet.

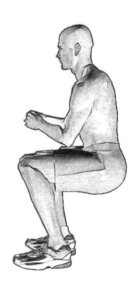

Starting Position   *Ending Position*

Day 1: Push-ups

Lie stomach down on the floor, feet together. Place your hands under your shoulders and push yourself up into a straight plank. Look forward and keep your back straight. Lower your body until either your torso or your chin touches the floor. Then push yourself up again. Inhale when you go down, exhale when you push yourself up. Add a score of 1 every time you cycle from the starting position to the ending position and back to the starting position.

Starting Position

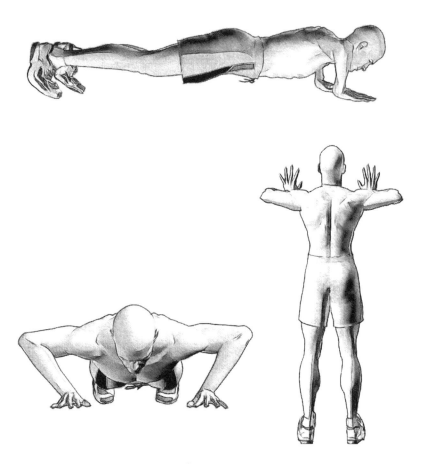

Ending Position

Day 1: Lunges

Stand in a straight and relaxed position. Step forward with your left foot and simultaneously bring your right knee down an inch from the floor so that your left quadriceps is horizontal with the ground. Push yourself back up to a standing position and start over with the other leg. Inhale as you go down; exhale as you push yourself back up. Add a score of 1 for every lunge you perform. If you lunge 5 times on the right and 5 times on the left, write down 10 on your log sheet.

Starting Position   *Ending Position*

Day 1: Plank Bridge

Lie face down on the ground and push yourself up onto your toes and elbows. Keep your back straight and your stomach tucked in. Don't let your hips go up and don't let your stomach sag. Look a foot in front of you. Hold this position for as long as you can. Your score is based on how long you can stay in the position with good form. If you hold the plank for 50 seconds, write down 50 on your log sheet.

Plank Bridge Position

Day 2: Elevated Push-ups

This is just like a simple pushup with your feet up on something. Use stair steps, a chair, a bench, a counter or anything you might have handy. Lower your body to your torso and push yourself back up to your starting position to complete the move. Inhale when you go down, exhale when you come up. Score it like standard push-ups.

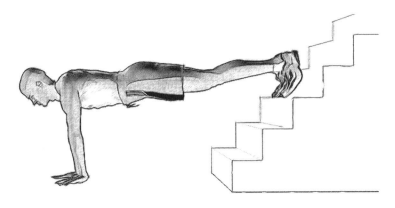

Starting Position

Ending Position

Day 2: Bird Dog

Get on your hands and knees and keep your back flat. Lift up your right leg back and your left arm forward until they form a straight horizontal line. Mark the position with a short pause and bring your leg and arm back down. Repeat with the opposite arm and leg. Breathe regularly. Add a score of one every time you cycle from starting to ending position and back to the starting position.

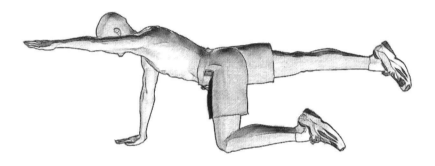

Starting Position

Ending Position

Day 2: Squat Pulses

First, put yourself in a squatting position with your legs bent and hands in front of your torso. Now pulse up and down 2 to 3 inches for as long as you can. Keep your back straight and look forward. Breathe regularly. Your score is based on how long you can keep pulsing with good form. If you can do it for 45 seconds, write down 45 on your log sheet.

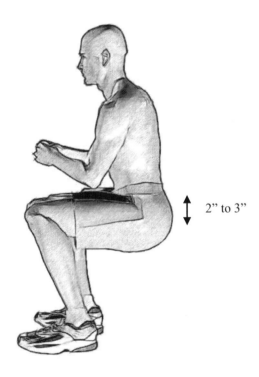

2" to 3"

Squat Pulses Position

Day 2: Superman

Lie face down on the floor with your arms straight out in front of your head. Simultaneously raise your legs and arms *as high as you can.* Keep your arms and legs straight. Hold the position for as long as possible. Breathe regularly. Your score is based on how long you can stay in the position with good form. If you hold the position for 20 seconds, write down 20 on your log sheet.

Superman Position

Day 3: Squat-Touch-Reach

Position your feet just a little over shoulder-width apart and put your arms straight in the air. While keeping your torso up, lower your body and your arms until you can touch the floor with your fingertips. Come back up to your starting position to complete the move. Inhale as you go down, exhale as you come back up. If you cycle through the move 30 times, log 30 on your log sheet.

Starting Position　　　　　　　　　*Ending Position*

Day 3: Reverse Lunges

Stand in a straight and relaxed position. Step back with your right foot and simultaneously bring your right knee down an inch from the floor so that your left quadriceps is horizontal with the ground. Push yourself back up to a standing position and start over with the other leg. Inhale as you go down; exhale as you push yourself back up. Add a score of 1 for every reverse lunge you perform. If you lunge 5 times on the right and 5 times on the left, write down 10 on your log sheet.

Starting Position   *Ending Position*

Day 3: Drop Squats

Position your feet shoulder-width apart and put your arms straight in the air. While keeping your torso up, hop into a down squat position with your feet spread 1 yard (3') apart and hands by your sides. Keep your back straight the whole time. Jump back into your starting position to complete the move. Inhale on your way down, exhale when you jump back up. Score it just like squats.

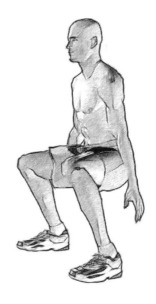

Starting Position   *Ending Position*

Day 3: Plank

Lay stomach down on the floor, feet together. Place your hands under your shoulders and push yourself up into a straight plank. Keep your back straight and your stomach tucked in. Look a foot in front of you. Hold this position for as long as you can. Your score is based on how long you can stay in the position with good form. If you hold the plank for 50 seconds, write down 50 on your log sheet.

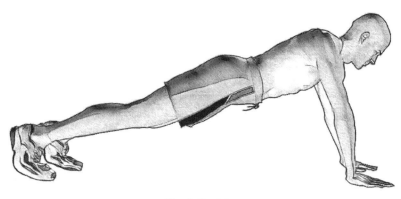

Plank Position

Pool 2 – Schedule & Exercises

First, write down your new body measurements. Below are the exercises you will be performing for the second pool. Log your results on this page as you complete the exercises.

Pool 2	Week 4 (Fifty-Ten)	Week 5 (Tabata)	Week 6 (T-Attack)
Day 1 Jump Squats	…	…	
Chair Lift	…	…	
Alternating Splits	…	…	… : …
Dips	…	…	
REST 1 DAY			
Day 2 Diamond Push-Ups	…	…	
Wall Squats	…	…	
Side Tri Rise	…	…	… : …
Mountain Climbers	…	…	
REST 1 DAY			
Day 3 Snowboarder's 180	…	…	
Plank In & Out	…	…	
Jump Kicks	…	…	… : …
Dive Bombers	…	…	

Body Measurements					
Resting heart rate	…	Chest	…	Buttocks	…
Weight	…	Left bicep	…	Left thigh	…
Waist	…	Right bicep	…	Right thigh	…

Day 1: Jump Squats

Position your feet just a little over shoulder-width apart with your arms relaxed at your sides. While keeping your torso up, lower your body until your thighs are parallel with the ground. At the same time, bring both your hands up in front of your torso. Keep your back straight the whole time. This is your starting position. Throw your hands down and jump as high as you can. Land back into a squat. Inhale on your way down, exhale when you push yourself back up. Score it just like standard squats. If you jump 10 times, log 10 on your sheet.

Starting Position   *Ending Position*

Day 1: Chair Lift

Side down on a chair or bench. Grab the base of the chair with both hands, one on each side (or both up front). Tighten your core and press against your hands to lift up your whole body. Breathe regularly and stay in this position for as long as possible. If you hold the Indian lift for 15 seconds, write down 15 on your log sheet

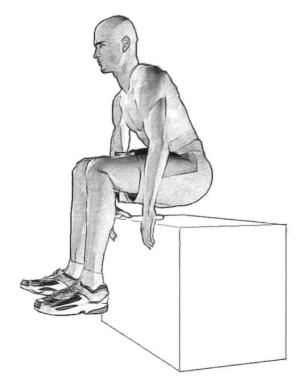

Chair Lift Position

Day 1: Alternating Splits

Lunge with your right foot forward, then jump into a left-foot lunge. Jump back into a right foot lunge and repeat until time runs out or you reach your goal. Exhale as you jump up, inhale as you land. Add a score of 1 for every lunge you perform. If you lunge 5 times on the right and 5 times on the left, write down 10 on your log sheet.

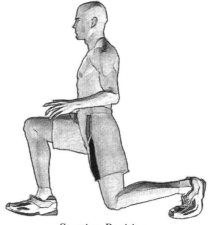

Starting Position

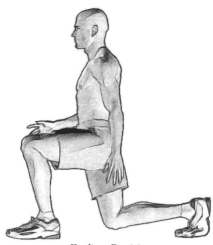

Ending Position

Day 1: Dips

Find an elevated surface such as a chair, bench, stool or coffee table. Face away from the elevated surface and grab its edge with both hands. Walk your feet forward until your body forms a straight line from shoulders to ankles. You are now in the starting position. To perform a dip, lower your body by bending your elbows to 90 degrees then push yourself back into the starting position. Inhale as you go down, exhale as you push up. Add a score of 1 every time you cycle from starting position to ending position.

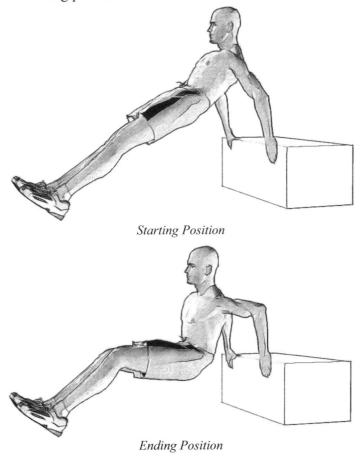

Starting Position

Ending Position

Day 2: Diamond Push-Ups

Make an L shape with your left hand and a reverse L shape with your right hand. Put your hands together so that your index fingers and your thumbs touch each other. This is a diamond shape. Put yourself into push-up position with your hands in the diamond shape under your chest. Lower your body, your heart should be right over the diamond shape. Push yourself back up to complete the move. Inhale when you go down, exhale when you come up. Score it like standard push-ups.

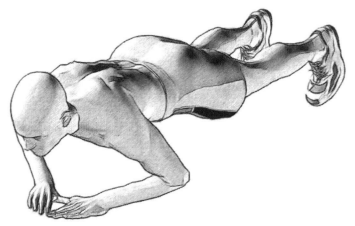

Diamond Push-Ups Position

Hands Position

Day 2: Wall Squats

Stand with your back against a wall and your feet shoulder width apart. Slide down the wall and walk your feet out until your knees are bent at 90 degrees. Let your arms hang by your side. Do not use your hands or arms to hold yourself. Stay in this position for as long as possible. Your score is based on how long you can stay in the position with good form. If you hold the wall squat for 40 seconds, write down 40 on your log sheet.

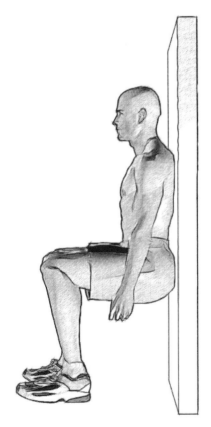

Wall Squat Position

Day 2: Side Tri Rise

Lie down on your right side. Place your right hand on your left shoulder and your left hand on the floor, under your right arm pit. Push up and straighten your arm to lift your upper body off the floor. Inhale when you go down, exhale when you come up. Add one point every time you cycle from starting to ending position. Alternate sides the following round.

Starting Position

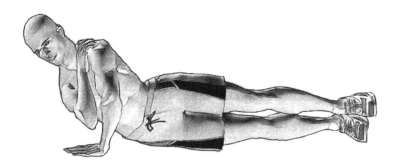

Ending Position

Day 2: Mountain Climbers

Start in a straight arms plank position. Bring your right knee towards your chest and put your foot on the ground. Your knee should be under your neck and your foot should be under your buttocks. Keep your left leg as straight as possible. Jump just high enough to shuffle your feet mid-air. When you land, your left leg will be in and your right leg will be straight out. Alternate your feet as fast as possible with good form. Breathe regularly. Score it like lunges.

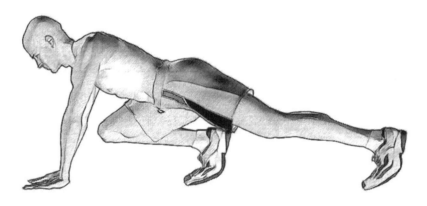

Starting Position

Ending Position

Day 3: Snowboarder's 180

For this exercise you will need a snowboard and some goggles. Nah, I'm just messing with you; a pulse and some determination will do just fine. While keeping your torso up, squat down until you can touch the floor with the tip of your left hand. This is your starting position. Jump 180 degrees and land squatted down with your right hand where your left hand just was. Jump back into your starting position to complete the move. Exhale as you jump and inhale as you land. Add a score of 1 every time you get airborne. If you jump 180 degrees 20 times, write down 20 on your log sheet.

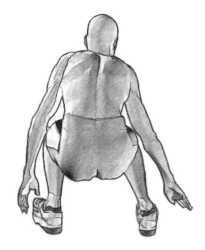

Starting Position   *Ending Position*

Day 3: Plank In & Out

Start in a straight-arms plank position. Jump your knees towards your chest with your feet under your buttocks. Jump back into a straight-arms plank to finish your move. Go as fast as you can with good form. Exhale as you jump in, inhale as you jump out. Add a score of 1 for every time you perform a full cycle: plank out to plank in and back to plank out.

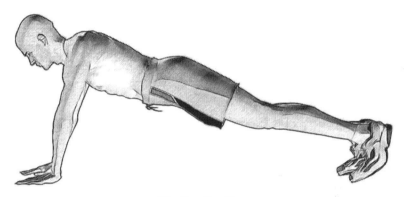

Starting Position

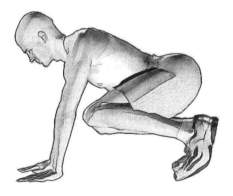

Ending Position

Day 3: Kick Jumps

Stand up and put your fists in front of your face as if you were protecting yourself in a boxing match. Kick your right leg up as high as you can. As you bring it back down, kick your left leg up. You should be in the air momentarily. Keep hopping and kicking as high and as fast as possible. Alternate legs every time you kick. This is a very rapid exercise so it's important that you breathe properly. Beware not to hyperextend your knees and keep your chest and head up. Add a score of 1 every time you kick your foot out.

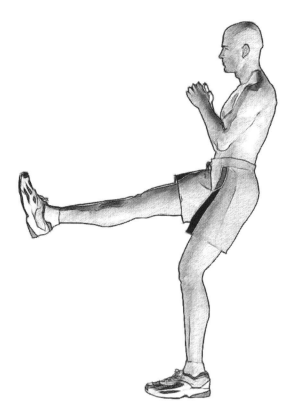

Kick Jumps Position

Day 3: Dive Bombers

To get in your starting position, put yourself in a straight-arms plank. Slowly walk your feet up towards your shoulders until your body forms an inverted V. Adjust your feet so that they are shoulder width apart. Now imagine there is a fence in front of you and dive under it. Point your upper body up as you come out from under the fence and straighten your arms. Reverse the movement to come back into your starting position. Breathe regularly. Add a score of 1 for every time you cycle from starting to ending position.

Starting Position

Ending Position

Pool 3 – Schedule & Exercises

Once again, write down your new body measurements. Here are the third pool's exercises. Log your results on this page as you complete the exercises.

Pool 3		Week 7 (Fifty-Ten)	Week 8 (Tabata)	Week 9 (T-Attack)
Day 1	Burpees	…	…	
	Cross Hops	…	…	
	Cliff Scalers	…	…	… : …
	Incline Dips	…	…	
	REST 1 DAY			
Day 2	Crocodile Push-Ups	…	…	
	Deck Squat Jumps	…	…	
	1 Leg Wall Squat	…	…	… : …
	Jack Knives	…	…	
	REST 1 DAY			
Day 3	High Knee Jumps	…	…	
	Wall Hand Walkouts	…	…	
	1 Leg Hip Bridges	…	…	… : …
	Invisible Chair	…	…	

Body Measurements					
Resting heart rate	…	Chest …		Buttocks	…
Weight	…	Left bicep …		Left thigh	…
Waist	…	Right bicep …		Right thigh	…

Day 1: Burpees

The burpee is one of the best full body exercises out there and my personal favorite. Start in a standing position and drop into a straight arms plank. Perform a push-up. Now hop your feet in towards your chest and jump up as high as you can. As you land, get yourself into a push-up and start all over again. Remember to breathe. Add a score of 1 for every time you cycle from the starting position to the ending position. If you do 10 burpees, log 10 on your sheet.

Starting Position   *Push-Up*

Knees In   *Ending Position*

Day 1: Cross Hops

From a stand, lift your left leg and balance all your weight onto your right leg. Now, hop forward, backward, left and right to form a cross with your foot. Stay on the ball of your foot the whole time, do not let your heel touch the ground. Cover as much distance as you can. Alternate foot on the next round. Breathe regularly. Add a score of 1 every time you complete a full cross.

Cross Hops Position

Day 1: Cliff Scalers

For this move, you will need a little more room than usual. Position yourself into a straight-arm plank. Perform one push-up. Then, keeping your arms and body straight, take two steps to the right, moving sideways like a crab. Perform another push-up. Take two steps to the left to get back into your starting position. Keep going as much as you can to get the highest score. Add a score of 1 for every push-up you perform. If you do one push-up, move to the right, do another push-up, move to the left and do a final push-up, write down 3 on your log sheet.

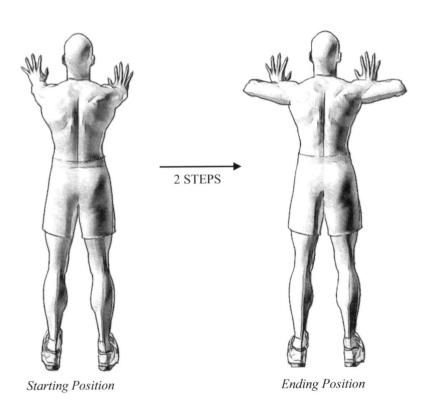

2 STEPS

Starting Position   *Ending Position*

Day 1: Incline Dips

For this exercise, you'll position your body the opposite of the dips: put your hands on the floor and your feet up on the elevated surface. To perform an incline dip, lower your body by bending your elbows to 90 degrees then push yourself back into the starting position. Inhale as you go down, exhale as you push up. Add a score of 1 every time you cycle from starting position to ending position.

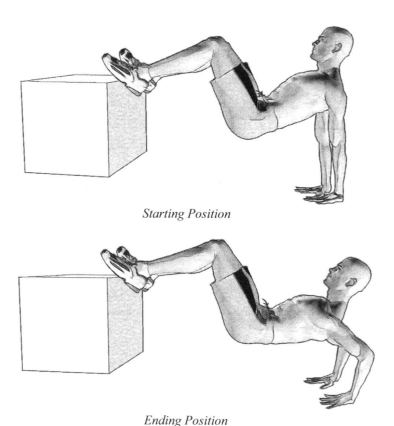

Starting Position

Ending Position

Day 2: Crocodile Push-Ups

Much like the cliff scalers, this is an advanced push-up exercise. But instead of stepping sideways in between push-ups, you'll be stepping forward and backward *as* you perform the push-ups. Get yourself into push-up position and take a step forward by advancing your right hand and your right leg. Now bring your left hand and your left leg forward to complete the second step. Keep going until you've taken 8 steps or you've run out of room. Then, do the same thing backwards to get back to your starting position. Keep your core tight and your back straight. Don't wuss out on the movement, bend your elbows at least 90 degrees every time. Inhale when you go down, exhale when you come up. Score it like standard push-ups.

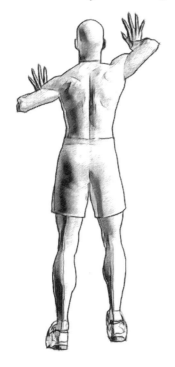

Starting Position

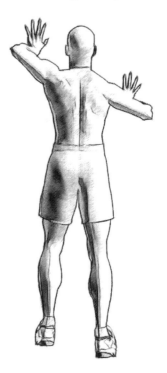

Ending Position

Day 2: Deck Squat Jumps

Stand up straight with 8 to 10 feet of room behind you. Jump up as high as you can. When you land, squat down until your glutes hit the floor and roll back. Bring your knees to your chest and straighten your legs so that your feet are behind your head. Without using your hands, roll forward until your feet touch the floor and jump up as high as you can. Breathe properly. Add one point every time you cycle from starting to ending position. Practice this move a few times before you start the routine.

Starting Position

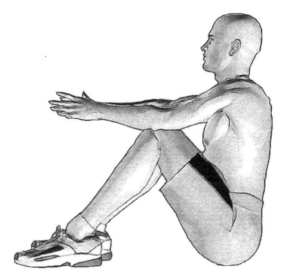

Middle Position

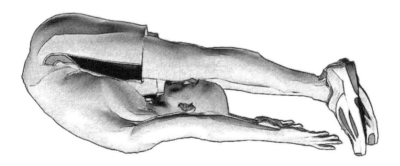

Ending Position

Day 2: 1 Leg Wall Squat

This is just like a standard wall squat except you'll be doing it on 1 leg. Start in a wall squat position and slowly raise your right leg until it's parallel to the floor. Don't use your hands. Keep this position for as long as possible. Take a pause if you need to, then get back into position. Your score is based on how long you hold the position in proper form, pauses don't count toward your score. Alternate legs on the next round.

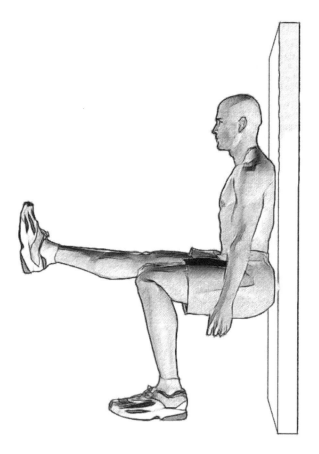

1 Leg Wall Squat Position

Day 2: Jack Knives

Let's build your shoulders. Put yourself in a straight-arms plank. Pivot your hands inward so that you're your fingers face each other. Slowly walk your feet up towards your shoulders until your body forms an inverted V. Now bend your arms until your head touches the floor. Keep your core tight. Push yourself back up into your starting position. Inhale as you go down, exhale as you push up. Add a score of one every time you cycle from starting to ending position.

Starting Position

Ending Position

Day 3: High Knee Jumps

This one's a killer. It'll get your quads burning and your heart racing. Start in a squat position with your hands by your sides. Simultaneously throw your hands up and jump as high as you can. As you reach the apex of your jump, bring knees up so that your thighs are parallel to the floor and slap your hands on your knees. Fall down to a squat and start over. Keep your back straight through the whole move. Exhale as you jump and inhale as you land. Take breaks when you need to. Add a score of 1 every time you slap your knees.

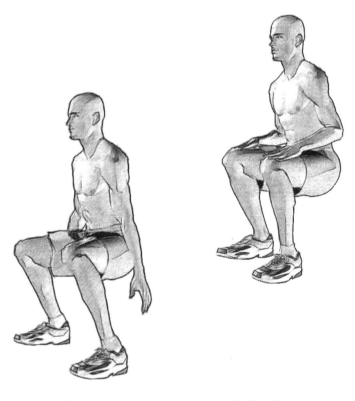

Starting Position   *Ending Position*

Day 3: Wall Hand Walkouts

Find a wall and put your back to it. Set yourself in a plank position with your hands on the floor and your feet on the wall. Keep your arms straight. Your body should be parallel to the floor. This is your starting position. Now walk back with your hands and feet until your body is almost vertical against the floor. Don't go too far or you'll lose your balance. Keep your body straight the whole time. Walk back down until your body is horizontal again. Breathe regularly. Add a score of 1 every time you perform a full cycle.

Alternative: If you find the move too hard, simply put yourself in a handstand and hold the position for as long as possible. Score it like a plank.

Starting Position

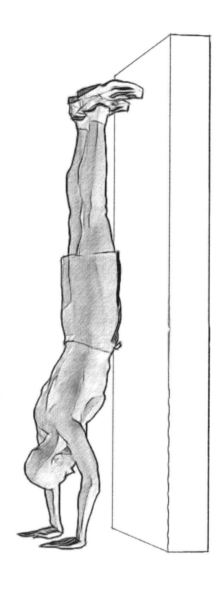

Ending Position

Day 3: 1 Leg Hip Bridges

Face a chair and sit down on the floor. Lay your back on the floor and put your feet on the base of the chair with your knees at 90 degrees. While keeping your left foot on the chair, lift your right foot in the air so that your left leg is straight. This is your starting position. Now raise your bottom until your leg and torso form a straight line. Come back down to finish the move. Alternate legs on the next round. Score every cycle.

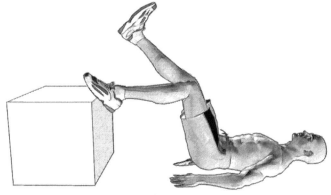

Starting Position

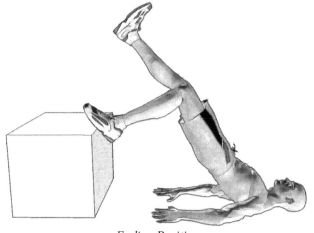

Ending Position

Day 3: Invisible Chair

Stand up straight with your feet a little more than shoulder-width apart. Raise your hands up in the air and slowly lower your body until your knees are at a 90 degree angle. Keep your chest up and look straight ahead. You should give the illusion that you are sitting on an invisible chair. Your score is based on how long you can stay in the position with good form. If you hold the invisible chair for 40 seconds, write down 40 on your log sheet.

Invisible Chair Position

Pool 4 – Schedule & Exercises

You've completed nine weeks of workouts so it's time to write down your new body measurements. Here are the final exercises. Log your results on this page as you complete the workouts.

Pool 4		Week 10 (Fifty-Ten)	Week 11 (Tabata)	Week 12 (T-Attack)
Day 1	Heel Touches	…	…	
	Pulse Ups	…	…	… : …
	Leg Over Crunches	…	…	
	Alternating Crunches	…	…	
	REST 1 DAY			
Day 2	Staggered Push-Ups	…	…	
	Sprinter's Squat	…	…	… : …
	Air Force Crunches	…	…	
	Lalanne Plank	…	…	
	REST 1 DAY			
Day 3	Table Kicks	…	…	
	Ski Jumps	…	…	… : …
	Butt Lifts	…	…	
	Handstand Push-ups	…	…	

Body Measurements					
Resting heart rate	…	Chest	…	Buttocks	…
Weight	…	Left bicep	…	Left thigh	…
Waist	…	Right bicep	…	Right thigh	…

Day 1: Heel Touches

Lie down on your back and bring your knees up so that your thighs are perpendicular to your calves. Put your hands palm down by your sides. Raise your shoulders slightly off the floor and look up to the ceiling. This is your starting position. Now use your abdominals to crunch up and touch your heels with your finger tips. Come back down to your starting position to complete the move. Exhale as you crunch up, inhale as you come back down. Add a score of 1 for every time you cycle from the starting position to the ending position. If you do 40 heel touches, log 40 on your sheet.

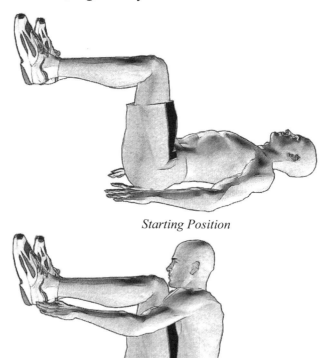

Starting Position

Ending Position

Day 1: Pulse Ups

Lie down on your back with your hands palm down by your sides. Bring your legs up until they are perpendicular to the floor. Fight to keep your legs as straight as possible. This is your starting position. Now use your abs to lift your legs towards the sky until your butt is off the floor. Keep your legs vertical. Once you've reached the apex, bring your legs and butt back down in a controlled manner. Breathe regularly. Add a score of 1 every time you cycle from starting to ending position.

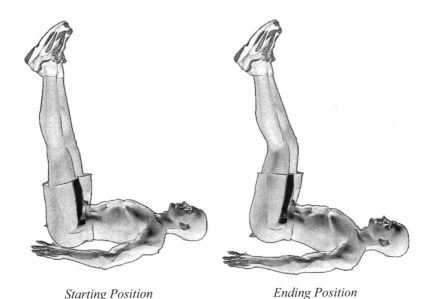

Starting Position   *Ending Position*

Day 1: Leg Over Reverse Crunches

Lie down on your back with your hands palm down by your sides. Bend your right knee enough so that your right foot can rest comfortably flat on the ground. Place your left leg over your right leg as if you were about to put your laptop on it. This is your starting position. Using your lower abs, pull your legs toward your chest. Go as far as you can and breathe regularly. Count 1 point for every time you cycle from starting to ending position.

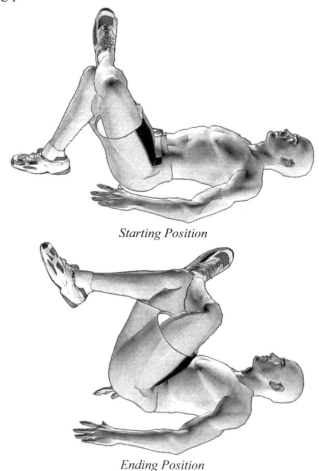

Starting Position

Ending Position

Day 1: Alternating Crunches

Lie down on your back and interlace your fingers behind your head. Bend your knees so that both your feet can comfortably rest flat on the ground. This is your starting position. Without moving your legs, simultaneously raise and twist your upper body toward your right knee. Come back down to your starting position before rising and twisting the other way. Exhale as you come up, inhale as you come back down. Add a score of 1 every time you crunch up.

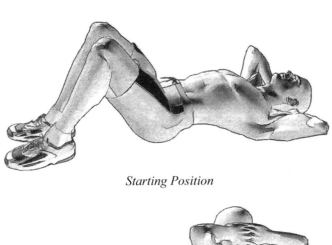

Starting Position

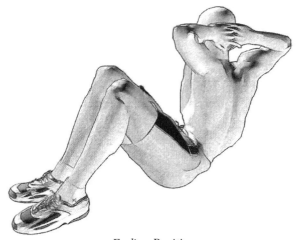

Ending Position

Day 2: Staggered Push-Ups

Ah, enough of the abs exercises! First, put yourself in a push-up position. Now move your right hand 1 hand-length forward and your left hand 1 hand-length backwards. Perform a push-up. Explode back up and shuffle your hands as you land. Your right hand is now at the back and your left hand is now forward. Keep going as fast as you can with good form. Breathe in as you go down, exhale as you explode up. Score it like standard push-ups.

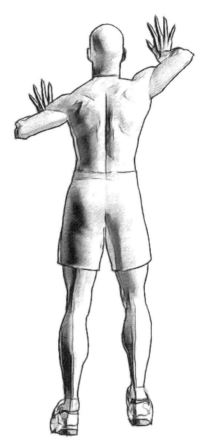

Staggered Push-Ups Position

Day 2: Sprinter's Squat

Stand straight and bend your right knee so that your right shin is parallel to the ground. Bring your hands up as if you were a boxer protecting himself. This is your starting position. Bend your left knee until your thigh is parallel to the ground and touch your left foot with your hands. Keep your right knee bent this whole time so that your right foot never touches the ground. Repeat the move with the same leg until your time is over or you've reached your reps goal. Inhale as you come down, exhale as your push yourself back up. Add 1 point for every sprinter's squat you perform. Alternate sides on the next round.

Starting Position   *Ending Position*

Day 2: Air Force Crunches

Lie down on your back and bend your knees so that your feet are flat on the ground. Place your hands across your chest with your fingertips touching your shoulders. Look up at the ceiling. While keeping your arms snug against your torso, contract your abdominals to lift your upper body off the floor. Keep going until your elbows touch your thighs. Lower yourself back down in a controlled manner. Add a score of 1 every time you complete a crunch.

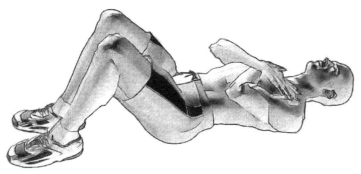

Starting Position

Ending Position

Day 2: Lalanne Plank

This move is based on Jack Lalanne's famous push-ups. First, put yourself in a straight plank position. Slide your hands forward until your body is completely straight and your torso is about 4" off the floor. Look at your hands. Hold this position as long as possible. If you need a break, slowly come down to your knees, gather yourself and then get right back into it. Breathe regularly. Score it like the standard plank.

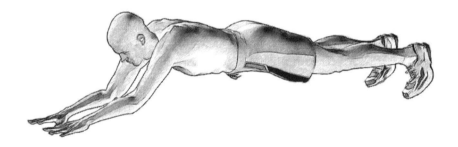

Lalanne Plank Position

Day 3: Table Kicks

Squat down until your hands reach the floor. Walk your hands back until you are in a table top position: knees bents at 90 degrees and arms straight under your shoulders. Kick your left leg up to a horizontal position. Bring your left leg back down and simultaneously kick your right leg up. Go as fast as you can and breathe regularly. Add a score of 1 every time you switch legs.

Starting Position

Ending Position

Day 3: Ski Jumps

Squat down and put your hands by your sides. Jump as high and far as you can to your *side*. Throw your hands up to help give yourself momentum on the jump. Land softly back into a squat. Repeat the move, this time jumping to the other side, to get back to your starting position. Inhale as you go down, exhale as you jump up. Add a score of one every time you jump.

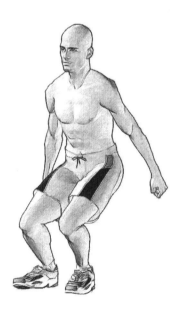
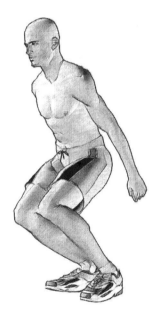

Starting Position   *Ending Position*

Day 3: Butt Lifts

Get on your hands and knees and keep your back flat. Lift up your right leg until it is parallel to the floor. This is your starting position. Using your left leg, raise your butt up as high as you can. Come back down to complete the move. Do not let your knee hit the floor on the way down. Add a score of 1 every time you perform a full cycle. Alternate legs on the next round.

Starting Position

Ending Position

Day 3: Handstand Push-Ups

Facing the wall, or facing away from the wall, put yourself in a hand stand position. Place your hands a little over shoulder-width apart and keep your body straight. Look in front of you. Bend your elbows until your head just touches the floor. Push yourself back up to your starting position. If you feel like you've reached your maximum, stop! We don't want you falling on your head. Add a score of 1 every time you cycle from starting to ending position. Inhale as you come down, exhale as you push yourself back up.

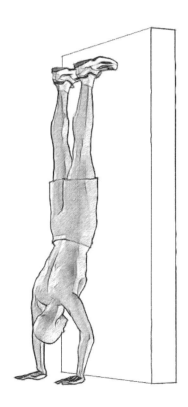
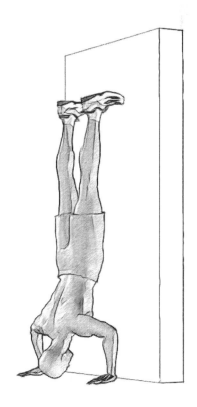

Starting Position   *Ending Position*

PART VI
The Meal Plan

The DIY Meal Plan

" Give a man a fish; you have fed him for today.
Teach a man to fish; and you have fed him for a lifetime. "
- Chinese Proverb

W HEN I ORIGINALLY WROTE THIS SECTION, I laid out a full multi-week meal plan, but then I realized you wouldn't learn much from it. Everybody's tastes are different and much of the meal plan would be wasted. So I scratched the whole thing. Instead, I'll show how I developed my own meal plan so that you can do the same.

First, I had to decide when and how often I would eat. As we saw earlier, how often you eat doesn't really matter so I based my decisions on convenience alone. I wake up at 6:00 every morning and because I haven't eaten since the night before, I like to eat my breakfast right after my shower. I'm also a social eater, so I eat lunch with my coworkers and dinner with my friends. We eat lunch around 12:30pm and dinner around 8:30pm. Now, I'm the kind of guy who gets hungry if he hasn't eaten for a few hours so I threw in a couple of snacks: one in the morning, for whenever I get hungry between breakfast and lunch, and one in the afternoon to break the 8 hour fast between my lunch and dinner. So I planned for three meals: breakfast, lunch, and dinner, and two snacks: one in the morning and one in the afternoon.

Meal	Food
Breakfast	...
Snack	...
Lunch	...
Snack	...
Dinner	...

Maybe you don't have time for snacks, in that case just eat three meals a day. Or perhaps you snack constantly, make it four snacks and two meals. All that matters is that it's convenient for you.

Every time I put food in my mouth, it needs to be balanced (Rule #3). So I drew myself a simple table to make sure I was getting everything I needed.

Carbs	Proteins	Fats	Produce
...	...	...	...

All you need to do is write down at least one item in each column. At this point, we're not even concerned with how much of what goes where. Just write in what you'd like to eat and we'll adjust the quantities later on. This is what my breakfast looks like:

Carbs	Proteins	Fats	Produce
Oatmeal	Eggs Ham Milk, whole	Walnuts	Blueberries

For my breakfast, I like to start with a bowl of blueberries and walnut oatmeal with milk and finish with a small ham omelet. Leverage the tables on pages 50 (protein), 52 (fats) and 55 (carbs) to come up with your own meals. Maybe you're more of a continental breakfast kinda guy or you you're an amateur of the fresh traditional Israeli breakfast... as long as you can fill in all four columns, you're on the right track. Repeat this exercise for your lunch, your dinner and your snacks. After you do it a few times, you'll get good at it pretty quickly. Once you're all set, you just need to adjust your portion sizes.

Plan for the Right Amount

"Plans are nothing; planning is everything."
- Dwight D. Eisenhower

O N PAGE 56, YOU CALCULATED how much food you need to eat every day. You also established how much of your food intake should be proteins, how much of it should be fats and how much of it should come from carbs. In the previous chapter, you planned to eat all of those macronutrients at every meal. Now, all you need to do is adjust your food intake quantities so that they match your goals. This is where a tool like LiveStrong's DailyPlate truly comes in handy. For the scope of this program, we're not too worried about how much of each nutrient you get per meal. Let's focus instead on achieving our goal for the day. If you want to break it down further than that, great, but you really don't have to.

My friend's goal was to eat 160 x 12 = 1920 calories per day. That's 160g of protein, 53g of fat and 200g of carbs. He created his meal plan, based on the previous chapter, and entered it on DailyBurn.com, another meal planner. The website presented him a pie chart with a summary of his numbers. He had underestimated his total calorie intake. Also, he had too much fat and not enough protein. So he adjusted his plan to reach his calorific goals. This is what he came up with:

Meal	Food
Breakfast	2 whole eggs, 1 egg white, 1 slice of bread, 2 cups of Greek yogurt, 1 glass of 2% milk.
Lunch	1 foot long double stacked roast beef sandwich, 1 orange. Water.
Dinner	1 red snapper fillet cooked in olive oil, 2 cups of spinach, 1 cup of white rice, 1 homemade strawberry smoothie. Water

That got him 159g of protein, 49g of fat and 218g of carbs for a total of 1949 calories. Close enough! You don't need to match your target exactly; you can give yourself some margin of error. Also, don't forget to drink your water!

Now you know how to come up with your own meals and plan for the right amount of food. That's enough skills and knowledge to feed yourself properly, but some days you might want to spice it up a bit and follow a real recipe.

ℬ · ℭ

Finding Recipes

*"The only two things I don't eat for breakfast
are lunch and dinner."*
- Author Unknown

LEAN GROUND BEEF, KIDNEY BEANS, TOMATOES AND ONIONS: that just screams Chili Con Carne. But what if you had selected chicken breast, quinoa, peppers and seeds? What could you prepare with that? Well, if nothing comes to mind, you can enlist the help of the internet!

You've probably heard of *AllRecipes.com*, it's the most popular recipes web site in the world. But did you know they offer a way to search for recipes by ingredient? Go to their homepage and click on "Ingredients" above the search box. That will take you to a page where you can enter all the ingredients you want to use in your recipe. For this example, type in "chicken", "quinoa", "pepper", and "seeds". Hit search. Ah, a quinoa salad and a quinoa soup come up. Okay, that's good, but you might not be in the mood for either of those today. Let's try something else, remove one of the ingredients in your list. Let's get rid of the seeds and run the query again. Hit search. Aha! Curried chicken quinoa! That sounds pretty tasty. Now all you need to do is make sure that the recipe follows the 5 principles of eating right. If it doesn't, can you modify it? You might need to add or remove ingredients from your meal plan. As long as you hit your target numbers, you'll be fine.

Most of the time you'll be able to come up with your own recipes from your meal plan. But for the times you get stuck, you can always reference AllRecipes.com for some fresh ideas.

ஐ · ಞ

Eating Communally

"The first thing you lose on a diet is your sense of humor."
- Author Unknown

TWO MONTHS A YEAR, my coworker refuses to join us for lunch, no matter how hard we try to invite him along. "Aw, I wish I could, but I'm on a strict diet," he says. He eats properly in January, following his New Year resolution, and June, just in time to go the beach. After 4 or 5 weeks, he usually falls off his diet because it's impossible to maintain both the diet and his social lifestyle at the same time.

You need to find a good balance between your nutrition and your social life; otherwise you will fall off the bandwagon. If you don't have a bodybuilding competition coming up in two weeks, odds are you can indulge a little bit without much side effect. A good way to find equilibrium is to monitor your progress with time. If you find that eating out three times a week and going to happy hour on Fridays is slowing down your progress too much, or even reversing it, then adjust accordingly. Get rid of happy hour, eat out only twice a week and see how that works out. Once you find something that works for you, jot it down. It will take you a little trial and error, but in the end you will be much happier for it.

℘ · ℛ

Final Thoughts

T ODAY, I CHALLENGED MYSELF to the US Army Physical Fitness Test (APFT). I aimed for a perfect score of 300 for the most challenging age group (27-31 years old). That meant performing 77 good form continual pushups, 82 military sit-ups and run two miles in under 13 minutes and 18 seconds. I asked my friend to join me, to verify my form and provide moral support. You know what? We both did it, and we both scored 300!

When I first started training, I knew I would become fitter, but I never thought I could gain so much strength in so little time. I entirely owe this incredible transformation to the principles laid out in this book. By spending less than an hour a week working out, I went from doing fewer than five push-ups at a time to getting a perfect score on the APFT. I went from being dead last in a 1k race to running 40 miles from the Google campus in Mountain View to Pier 1 in San Francisco.

Now that you've read this far, you know as much as I do and you have everything you need to transform your body for the better. It is now up to you to commit to the Max Capacity Training approach laid out in this book. So, set up your training schedule on your calendar, go buy some real food and get started already. A year from now you'll look back to this day and one of two things will happen: you will smile at how much you've accomplished for yourself or you will frown in frustration for abandoning your own goals. I hope to see you grin proudly!

ℰ · ℛ

Index

References

[1] Tipton KD, Ferrando AA. Improving muscle mass: response of muscle metabolism to exercise, nutrition and anabolic agents. Essays Biochem. 2008;44:85-98.

[2] Rooney KJ, Herbert RD, Balnave RJ. Fatigue contributes to the strength training stimulus. Med Sci Sports Exerc. 1994 Sep;26(9):1160-4.

[3] Lawton T, Cronin J, Drinkwater E, Lindsell R, Pyne D. The effect of continuous repetition training and intra-set rest training on bench press strength and power. J Sports Med Phys Fitness. 2004 Dec;44(4):361-7.

[4] Tran QT, Docherty D, Behm D. The effects of varying time under tension and volume load on acute neuromuscular responses. Eur J Appl Physiol. 2006 Nov;98(4):402-10.

[5] Medrano IC, Muscular failure training in conditioning neuromuscular programs. J. Hum Sport Exerc. 2010 May;5(2):196-213

[6] de Salles BF, Simão R, Miranda F, Novaes Jda S, Lemos A, Willardson JM. Rest interval between sets in strength training, Sports Med. 2009;39(9):765-77

[7] Martin JG. High-intensity Interval Training: A Time-efficient Strategy for Health Promotion. Current Sports Medicine Reports 2007, 6:211-213

[8] Kirsten A. Burgomaster, Krista R. Howarth, Stuart M. Phillips, Mark Rakobowchuk, Maureen J. MacDonald, Sean L. McGee and Martin Gibala. Similar metabolic adaptations during exercise after low volume sprint interval and traditional endurance training in humans. J Physiol 586: 151-160, 2008

[9] Tremblay, A. et al. Impact of exercise intensity on body fatness and skeletal muscle metabolism. Metabolism.1994; 43(7): 814-818.

[10] Izumi Tabata; Kouji Nishimura, Hirai Motoki, Futoshi Ogita, Motohiko Miyachi, Kaoru Yamamoto, Effects of moderate-intensity endurance and high-intensity intermittent training on anaerobic capacity and VO2max. Japan Medicine & Science in Sports & Exercise. 28(10):1327-1330, October 1996.

[11] Shellock F. Physiological Benefits of Warm-up. Physician Sportsmen 11:134-139, 1983) p207

[12] Shyne K, Dominquez. To Stretch or not to Stretch? The physician Sportsmed 10:137-140, 1982

[13] Houmard JA Jones Jones, RA, Smith LL, Wells JM, Kobe RW, McGooan SA. The effects of Warm-up and responses to intense exercise. Int J Sports Med 10:12:480-483, 1991

[14] Iris Shai, Meir J Stampfer. Weight-loss diets—can you keep it off? American Journal of Clinical Nutrition, Vol. 88, No. 5, 1185-1186, November 2008

[15] Hartman JW, Tang JE, Wilkinson SB, Tarnopolsky MA, Lawrence RL, Fullerton AV, Phillips SM. Consumption of fat-free fluid milk following resistance exercise promotes greater lean mass accretion than soy or carbohydrate consumption in young novice male weightlifters. American Journal of Clinical Nutrition, 2007;86:373-381.

[16] DJ Jenkins et al. Glycemic index of foods: a physiological basis for carbohydrate exchange. Am J Clin Nutr, 1981; 34: 362–366

[17] Adult Weight Management (AWM) Low Glycemic Index Diets. In American Dietetic Association Evidence Library web site. Retrieved from http://www.adaevidencelibrary.com/template.cfm?template=guide_summary&key=626

[18] Das et. Al. Long-term effects of 2 energy-restricted diets differing in glycemic load on dietary adherence, body composition, and metabolism in CALERIE: a 1-y randomized controlled trial. Am J Clin Nutr. 2007 Apr;85(4):1023-30SK

[19] Bellisle F, McDevitt R, Prentice AM. Meal frequency and energy balance. Br J Nutr. 1997 Apr;77 Suppl 1:S57-70

[20] Das et. Al. Long-term effects of 2 energy-restricted diets differing in glycemic load on dietary adherence, body composition, and metabolism in CALERIE: a 1-y randomized controlled trial. Am J Clin Nutr. 2007 Apr;85(4):1023-30SK

[21] Price, Weston A. Nutrition and Physical Degeneration: A Comparison of Primitive and Modern Diets and Their Effects 1939. Paul B. Hoeber, Inc; Medical Book Department of Harper & Brothers.

[22] Yamashita, S., et al. 2006. Effects of music during exercise on RPE, heart rate and the autonomic nervous system. The Journal of Sports Medicine and Physical Fitness, 46 (3), 425–30

[23] Priest, D.L., Karageorghis, C.I., & Sharp, N.C. 2004. The characteristics and effects of motivational music in exercise settings: The possible influence of gender, age, frequency of attendance, and time of attendance. The Journal of Sports Medicine and Physical Fitness, 44 (1), 77–86.

1364760R00087

Made in the USA
San Bernardino, CA
12 December 2012